Karl Marx

Karl Marx
Biographical Memoirs

BY

WILHELM LIEBKNECHT

LONDON
THE JOURNEYMAN PRESS

First German edition published Nuremberg, 1896
English translation published 1901
Reprinted by the Journeyman Press, 1975
97 Ferme Park Road
Crouch End
London N8 9SA

ISBN 0 904526 05 4

Printed in Great Britain by Compton Printing Ltd,
Aylesbury and bound by Ebenezer Baylis & Son Ltd,
Worcester

TRANSLATOR'S NOTE.

In my translation I have endeavored to preserve as much of the delightful freshness and
racy strength of Liebknecht's style as I could
without doing violence to the spirit of the English language. If I have succeeded in saving
enough of the charm of the original to make the
reader forget that he is reading a translation I
shall be well awarded for my exertions. For I
shall then feel that the English-speaking comrades, while coming closer to Marx through
Liebknecht, are brought nearer to Liebknecht
by me. What better recompense could I find?

E. UNTERMANN

December, 1900,

AUTHOR'S PREFACE.

"Better is the enemy of Good" is an old commonplace, but like most commonplaces, it nevertheless contains a truth, behind which I retire for shelter in presenting the following little book. A hundred times I have been asked to write about Marx and my personal relations to him, but I have always declined to do so. And declined from—how shall I call it?—a certain holy awe—or how shall I express myself more correctly?—from reverence of Marx. Noblesse oblige. And a Marx imposes weighty obligations. Could I do him justice? Had I the ability? Had I the time? Under the continually growing pressure of work I was condemned to haste, to superficial working. And a eulogistic daubery, with Marx for its object, that would be an insulting lack of respect.

But I was being pressed harder and harder; my hesitation was met by the arguments, that a quickly executed sketch need not necessarily be a eulogistic daubery; that I should be able to say a good many things about and of Marx that nobody else could say; that anything bringing Marx nearer to our workers, to our party, would be valuable; and that in a case where there was only a choice between an incomplete publication of the sort that I alone could offer, or nonpublication of what I was able to say, the former surely deserved preference—even though it were only the lesser of two evils.

And finally, I had to admit this myself. In the meantime, Engels also has died; the only one who was associated nearly as much and as intimately as myself with Marx, the man and his family, during the London exile up to the beginning of the sixties. From the summer of 1850 until the beginning of the year 1862, when I felt a longing to return to Germany, I was almost daily and for years nearly all day in the house of Marx, forming a part of his family. Of course, many others besides myself found admission there. For naturally the house of Marx—consisting before he moved into the cottage of Maitland Park Road, of a modest floor in modest Dean street, Soho Square—was a pigeon-loft, where a multitude of various Bohemian, fugitive and refugee folk went in and out, little, great and greatest animals. It was furthermore the natural center of all settled comrades. True, a settled abode was a very elusive possibility. In London it was extremely difficult to obtain a secure livelihood, and the hunger drove most of the fugitives into the country or to America, providing it did not make short work by giving to the poor devil of a fugitive, if not an abode, at least a permanent place in a London graveyard. I lived through it, and I was, with the exception of the faithful Lessner and the no less faithful Lochner, who, however, could only come less frequently, the only one of the London "community" who, during the whole time—with only a short interruption to be mentioned later in the sketches—frequented the house of "MOHR"* (negro)—the nickname of Marx—like a member of the family. Under these circumstances, one cannot help learning and seeing more than others.

Marx, the man of science, the editor of the "Rheinische Zeitung" (Journal of the Rhine), one of the founders of the "Deutsch-Franzoesischen Jahrbuecher" (German-French Annals), one of the authors of the Communist Manifesto, the creator of "Capital"—this Marx belongs to publicity, he stands forth before the whole world, the target of criticism, challenging critique, not hiding the smallest wrinkle to the searching eye—were I to attempt writing about this Marx, then I should be guilty of a reckless

*The coal black hair, mustache and beard of Marx carned this nickname for him.—Translator.

imprudence indeed, for that is not feasible in the short minutes I can filch and wrest from the unavoidable work of the day and the hour. Such a task requires scientific penetration, and whence take the time necessary for it? Once, indeed, I had the fond craze—I came near saying craziness—that a life of science could be united to a life of strife, and I designed far-reaching plans; but soon I learned that we cannot serve two masters, nor two mistresses, either—and politics is a very exacting mistress, who abides no other gods near herself. I had to choose—either the one or the other—and those fond projects dissolved like misty phantoms. And that choice was surely the hardest I was ever called upon to make in my life! Even to this day I have moments of remorse.

Marx also had to choose—it was after the downfall of the commune, and the International Workingmen's Association which he had called into existence claimed so much of his strength, that his scientific work suffered in consequence. The perfection of his main work, the work of his life, was out of the question, if he remained in the leadership of the International Working-men's Association. He had to come to a decision, and he resigned the leadership of the International Workingmen's Association that in its old form had really fulfilled its mission and could not yet assume at that time the greater, wider, world-encircling form it has now. Since a dissolution of the I. W. A. would have had the appearance of a cowardly retreat and whereas the association, deprived of all opportunity for glorious action by the condition of the times, was in danger of being degraded to a hotbed for paltry and low intrigues, it was decided in 1872, at the Congress of the Hague, to remove it to the United States of North America, where there was no danger of such unworthy practices defiling the high goal. I was really not at all satisfied with this cure suggestive of Dr. Eisenbart—together with Bebel I was at that period serving a term in Hubertusburg—but later I gained the conviction that this decision had been a necessity for Marx, and without Marx at the head, the I. W. A. could not remain in Europe.

I shall not, then, treat in these sketches—except in the biographic sketch—the Marx of Science and the Marx of Politics, or I shall at the most throw passing sidelights on him. The picture of this Marx stands clearly forth for everybody; I shall try to reproduce Marx the man as I have come to know him.

And I believe, even if am but able to do this

incompletely, piece by piece, incoherently and
hastily, that it will still be better than not doing
it at all. And this gives me the courage to drive
off the thought of something better I cannot
realize, try as best I may, and to give that
which I can give. Even if it is not good, it is at
least better that I should give it, instead of
keeping this little contribution to the drawing of
a complete picture of Marx buried in my
memory.

And finally, is it not a duty as well I am fulfilling?

＊　＊　＊　＊　＊　＊　＊　＊　＊

Marx is such a man of science as has not been
produced a second time by this century, with the
exception of Darwin; he has the renown—and
the truly well-earned renown—of a great scholar.
His main works are written in a manner requiring, in order to be understood, a trained thinking, such as the mass of the workingmen do not
and cannot possess to-day. Thus Marx is standing, especially since he has not been much in
direct contact with the masses, in an elevated
position removing him personally from the people. The proletarians of all countries, to whose
emancipation he has devoted his life and on
whom he has bestowed the armament for their
revolutionary self-assistance, know him almost

solely as the man of science and as the author of the Communist Manifesto and founder of the International Workingmen's Association; about his private life, about himself as a person, a man, they know next to nothing. Hitherto only his adversaries have had their say about Marx the man, and working from a common model, they have pictured him as heartless, coldly calculating, looking down haughtily on the common people, that have served only as stepping stones to his ambition, from the eyrie of his contempt for men and the world.

How different was this man! And to bring him close to the people just as he was as a man, among his friends, in his family with wife and children, to show this generous heart together with his great mind—this generous heart that throbbed so warmly for everything human and for everything bearing human features—that is surely an act of justice and at the same time a useful task. I am not a Boswell who made a note of every word and of every movement of his idol, Johnson, as soon as he came home. I have never had any idols. Happily I became acquainted with great men so early and so intimately that my belief in idols and human gods was destroyed at a very early period, and even Marx was never an idol to me, although of all human beings I have ever met in my life he was the only one who has made an imposing impression on me.

But I have been associated with him more than a decade, in a time full of import, and at an age where we are most susceptible to deep and lasting impressions; I was his pupil in the narrower and wider sense of the word; I was his friend and confidant; I was, even after my return from England, in continued and intimate intercourse with him and his family; and the picture he has imprinted on my soul is so clear and fresh that I may well hope not to lose very much of its likeness and vividness in transferring it to paper. And if the saying, longing and love (pectus) make an orator, is true of a narrator as well, then I must succeed. True, there's that blessed "noblesse oblige." How to satisfy that!

However, no more hesitations. The black care that another might have done better, that perhaps I might have done better myself, shall not flutter around me any longer. Begone! And to work!   W. LIEBKNECHT.

End of March, 1896.

KARL MARX.

MAY 5, 1818—MARCH 14, 1883.

On the 5th of May, 1818, at Treves—the oldest German town—among the monuments of Roman civilization and amid the recent traces of the French Revolution that had cleaned the Rhenish province of medieval rubbish, a son was born in a Jewish family: Karl Marx. Only four years had passed since the province of the Rhine had been occupied by Prussia, and the new masters hastened, in the service of the "Holly Alliance," to replace the Heathenish-French by a Christian-German spirit. The pagan Frenchmen had proclaimed the equal rights of all human beings in the German Rhineland, and had removed from the Jews the curse of a thousand years of persecution and oppression, had made citizens and human beings of them. The Christian-German spirit of the "Holy Alliance" condemned the Heathenish-French spirit of equalization and demanded the renovation of the old curse.

Shortly after the birth of the boy, an edict was issued leaving to all the Jews no other choice but to be baptized or to forego all official position and activity.

The father of Marx, a prominent Jewish lawyer and notary public at the county court, submitted to the unavoidable, and, with his family, adopted the Christian faith.

Twenty years later, when the boy had grown to be a man, he gave the first reply to this act of violence in his pamphlet on the Hebrew question. And his whole life was a reply and was the revenge.

"Marx's father," writes Marx's daughter, "was a man of great talent, and thoroughly imbued with the French ideas of the eighteenth century concerning religion, science and art; his mother was descended from Hungarian Jews who had settled in Holland in the seventeenth century. Among his earliest friends and companions were Jenny—later his wife—and Edgar von Westphalen. It was their father—a half Scot—who inspired Marx with his first love for the romantic school; and while his father read Voltaire and Racine to him, Westphalen read Homer and Shakspeare to him. And these ever remained his favorite authors. Loved and feared by his schoolmates—loved, because he was always ready for boyish pranks, and feared because he wrote cutting, satirical poetry and exposed his enemies to derision, he then went through the customary school course and entered the university—first Bonn, then Berlin—where he studied law for a while to please his father, and history and philosophy to please himself."

In 1842 he planned to establish himself at the University of Bonn as lecturer of philosophy, but his friend of Berlin times, Bruno Bauer, who was private lecturer there and had no end of trouble with the higher authorities, advised him not to do so; and when Bruno Bauer was subjected to forcible measures during the year, the plan came to a natural end. In the meantime, a more fertile field had opened for the young Marx—a field for practical action. The Rhenish bourgeoisie, at that time of oppositional and decidedly liberal sentiments, the Camphausen's and Hansemann's, sought a connection with this young man of 24, whose extraordinary talent they had recognized. They founded a newspaper at the head of which he was placed in the fall of 1842, the "Rheinische Zeitung."

The editorship was a continual fight with the censorship that was still in vogue in Germany. "But," writes Engels, "the censorship could not get away with the 'Rheinische Zeitung.'" The wonderful ability of Marx to win and dominate men, already stood the test here. The censors allowed many passages to slip through that offended in Berlin; they received rebuke after rebuke. Finally, when censor after censor had been used up, the dangerous paper was submitted to double censorship; that of the censor and the further censorship of the president of the provincial government. But even that was ineffectual. Thoughts are not prehensible like butterflies. And the government, arrived at the end of its Latin, resorted to force and, in March, 1843, suppressed the "Rheinische Zeitung."

Marx, who a short time before had married the playmate of his childhood, Jenny von Westphalen, the sister of the future reactionary Prussian minister, von Westphalen, and the sister-in-law of the Jesuit father and Christian social demagogue, Florencourt, now took up his abode in Paris, where he united with Arnold Ruge for the publication of the "Deutsch-Franzoesischen Jahrbuecher. In these annals he published a lengthy essay on Hegel's legal philosophy and another one on the Hebrew question. It becomes manifest from both of them that he has found his way out of the heaven of a philosophy which is really only purged theology to the firm ground of facts and to socialism. He was now through with Hegelian philosophy. And from now on the development and activity of Marx

are heading straightway for that which is known
to us as his doctrine and which has gained
classic, perfect expression in "Capital."

The "Deutsch Franzoesischen Jahrbuecher"
lived only a short time, and copies of them are
almost unobtainable now. It may not be amiss,
therefore, to quote from them the following letter of the fiery young spirit.. (M. is Marx and R.
is Ruge):

"M. to R., on the treckschuit* to D., March,
1843:

"I am now traveling in Holland. So far as I
can gather from indigenous and French newspapers, Germany is stuck deep in the mud and
is getting down into it deeper and deeper. I
assure you, although one is feeling nothing less
than national pride, one still feels national
shame, even in Holland. The most inferior
Dutchman is yet an intelligent citizen compared
to the greatest German. And the opinions of
foreigners about the Prussian government!
There is an awe-inspiring agreement of opinions,
nobody is deceived any longer about this system and its simple nature. Some good, then,
has been accomplished by the new school of
thought. The gorgeous drapery of liberalism is
dropped, and the most detestable despotism

---

*Hollandish canal boat.

stands forth in its real nudity, visible to the eyes of the whole world.

"This is also a revelation, although reversed. It is a truth showing us at least the hollowness of our patriotism, the nature of our administration, and teaching us to hide our faces. You regard me smiling and ask: 'What does it avail? You don't start a revolution with shame.' I reply: Shame is already a revolution; it is really the victory of the French Revolution over the German patriotism that defeated it in 1813. Shame is a kind of wrath turned inwardly. And if a whole nation were really ashamed of itself, it would be the lion crouching down for the leap. I admit, even the shame is not yet present in Germany; on the contrary, those miserables are still patriots. But what system would take the patriotism out of them, if not this ridiculous one of the new knight? The comedy of despotism enacted with us is just as dangerous for him as the tragedy was once upon a time for the Stuarts and the Bourbons. And even if for a long time this comedy should not be taken for what it really is, it would still be a revolution. The state is too serious a thing to be turned into a buffoonery. Perhaps you could let a vessel full of fools drift before the wind a good while; but it would be drifting toward its fate, just because the fools would not believe it. This fate is the impending revolution."

This is the letter showing Marx in his storm and stress period, eager for fight in the battles of the present and looking keenly ahead into the future. Already he scents the morning air of revolution.

As a sample—a sample of his style, too—let me quote the conclusion of his essay on the Hebrew question:

"Christianity is the sublime thought of Judaism; Judaism is the common application of Christianity, but this application could become general only after Christianity as a complete religion had theoretically accomplished the self-estrangement of Man from himself and Nature.

"Now for the first time Judaism could gain universal supremacy and change dispossessed Man and Nature into disposable, salable objects, a prey to the serfdom of egoistic wants, of barter.

"Disposal is the practice of dispossession. Just as Man, while he is religiously handicapped, knows no better way to make his being objective, than to change it into a strange, phantastic being, so under the supremacy of egoistic want he can only manifest himself practically, produce practical objects, by submitting his products as well as his activity to the supremacy of a strange being and giving them the meaning of a strange being—of money.

"The Christian egoism of salvation in its practical completion naturally changes into the bodily egoism of the Jew, the celestial longing into the material, the subjectivism into egotism. We do not explain the tenacity of the Jew with his religion, but rather with the human cause of his religion, the practical want, the egoism.

"Because the real being of the Jew in civilized society has generally materialized, has become worldly, therefore civilized society could not convince the Jew of the unreality of his religious being which is in fact only the ideal conception of the practical want. Hence in the Pentateuch or in the Talmud, as well as in modern society, we find the real nature of the modern Jew, not as an abstract, but as an extremely empirical being, not alone as the limitation of the Jew, but also as the Jewish limitation of society.

"As soon as society will succeed in suspending the empirical character of Judaism, the barter and its preliminary causes, the Jew will become impossible, because his consciousness will be left without an object, because the subjective base of Judaism, the practical want, will be humanized, because the conflict between the sensual existence of the individual and the generic existence of the race will be over.

"The social emancipation of the Jew is the emancipation of society from the Jew."

To the language of the Hegelian school still used by Marx in this essay, the reader may reconcile himself as best he can. The course of reasoning is clear to everybody. Marx conceives the Hebrew question as an economic question, as a capitalistic question. The persecution of Jews—the name of Antisemitism had not yet become fashionable—is simply the competitive envy of Christian barter directed against Jewish barter, and not until human society emancipates itself from this spirit of barter, i. e., expressed in modern language of "Capitalism," will the Jew be emancipated, like all the rest of humanity and nations.

Here we have already the thought of the Communist Manifesto, of the International Workingmen's Association.

During his relations with the "Deutsch Franzoesischen Jahrbuecher," Marx became acquainted with Engels who, two years younger than himself, had gained by his stay in England a stronger materialistic conception of things and had "dishegeled" himself thoroughly. Both supplemented each other admirably; this they understood and, equal in spite of their difference, they formed that union: a union of friendship and union of work—of political and scientific work—unparalleled in its kind and never for a moment loosened or even disturbed—a union into which both of them carried their enormous power and in which both of them developed, strengthened and fully applied it.

After the discontinuance of the "Deutsch Franzoesischen Jahrbuecher," Marx and Engels worked together with Heine, Ewerbeck and others on the Paris "Vorwaerts" (Advance). As a sort of first pronunciamento of their new union, they wrote in collaboration the "Holy Family." This magnificent pamphlet—entirely out of print, I regret to say—is directed "against Bruno Bauer and consorts" and is, in the language of Engels, "a satirical critique of one of the last forms into which the German philosophical idealism of that time had strayed."

Marx who occupied himself in Paris mainly with the study of Political Economy (strange to say, called National Economy in Germany, just as if there were anything national in Political Economy!) and of the French Revolution, was at the same time engaged in a continuous war of the pen against the Prussian government. The latter revenged itself by securing from

Guizot, at that time the all-powerful minister of the "citizen king," his expulsion from France.

Marx now went to Brussels, where he helped to establish a workingmen's club and where, besides occasional contributions to the "Deutsche Bruesseler Zeitung" (German Brussels News), he continued his studies. At the freetraders' congress of 1846 he made a "Speech on Freetrade" that was published as a pamphlet in French; and he wrote against Proudhon's book, "The Philosophy of Misery"—La Philosophie de la Misere—his "Poverty of Philosophy"—Misere de la Philosophie—showing already the complete Marx and belonging, although originally written in French, to our party literature.

In Brussels, Marx and his friends entered the Communist Alliance, with the leaders of which he had held intercourse in Paris. It had become clear to him that the revolution could only emanate from the workingmen. In his essay on "The Critique of Hegel's Legal Philosophy," he had already proclaimed that the proletariat alone was capable of breaking the class rule, because it contained no class and in consequence nothing that could be suppressed. But in Germany the economic conditions were not yet sufficiently developed. No proletariat was ready there. "The proletariat," he writes on page 84,

"Just commences to form in Germany through the impending industrial movement; for it is not the naturally evolved, but the artificially produced poverty, not the human mass mechanically reduced by the weight of society, but created by its acute dissolution, especially by the dissolution of the middle class, that forms the proletariat; although it is self-evident that the natural poverty and the Christian German serfdom also will enter its ranks by degrees."

The fundamental conception of "Capital" in embryo!

The Communist Alliance had been founded in 1836 by German fugitives in Paris. "Up to the entrance of Marx a more or less conspiratory society, the alliance now transformed itself"—writes Engels who, of course, was "in it"—"into a simple organization for the communist propaganda, secret only by force of circumstances, the first organization of the German Social Democratic party. The alliance existed wherever there were German workingmen's clubs; in nearly all the German clubs of England, Belgium, France and Switzerland, and in very many clubs in Germany, the leading members belonged to this alliance, and the part played by the alliance in the growing movement of German workingmen was very important. At the same time our alliance was the first one to emphasize the international character of the entire labor movement and to put it into practice by admitting Englishmen, Belgians, Hungarians, Poles to membership and by calling international workingmen's meetings, especially in London."

About the character of the Communist Alliance, Marx himself has repeatedly made statements, principally in the "Disclosures about the Communists' Process" and in "Herr Vogt."

The German workingmen's clubs in foreign countries were before 1848 veritable high schools of socialism or communism, as it was called then.

"The transformation of the alliance"—Engels continues—"was accomplished in two congresses held in 1847, the second of which decided on the compilation and publication of the party principles in a manifesto to be edited by Marx and Engels."

This was the origin of the "Manifesto of the Communist Party," published for the first time in 1848, shortly before the February Revolution, and since translated into nearly all the European languages.

The Communist Manifesto I do not discuss. It is the cornerstone of the modern labor movement—it is its program as "Capital" later became its text-book.

The Manifesto is the work of Marx and Engels. What was supplied by the one, what by the other? An idle question! It is of one mould, and Marx and Engels are one soul—as inseparable in the Communist Manifesto as they remained to their death in all their working and planning, and as they will be to humanity in their works and creations while human beings are living on earth.

And the credit to have originated this Manifesto, to have provided through it a guide of thought and action, the fundamental principles of doctrine and tactics, for the proletariat—this credit is so colossal that even by dividing it in halves both of them still receive a giant's share.

If Marx and Engels had never created anything else, if they had been devoured by the revolution, on the eve of which they thundered forth into the world with prophetic vision the Manifesto—they had gained immortality.

* * * * * * * * *

The Manifesto had appeared at the beginning of February, 1848—on February 22 the old crater of revolution reopened after eighteen years of rest; on February 24 the July-throne was burned in front of the July-column on the Bastille square, and the July-column was once again for a short time a "Column of Liberty."*

The revolution had arrived and made its rounds. In Brussels it caused stormy demonstrations. The Belgian government which had previously refused several requests of the Prussian government to forbid a longer stay of that disagreeable Marx, had Marx arrested and transported across the frontier. He hastened to Paris, whither an invitation of his friend Flocon, editor-in-chief of the radical "Reforme" and member of the provisional government, had called him on the 25th of February. In Paris he quickly found his bearings and took part in the events to the best of his powers—but he opposed the attempts of Herwegh to create disturbances. However, Marx did not like it long in Paris. The news from Germany irresistibly drew him over there. Now his field of revolutionary activity was here. He returned to Cologne in March with the plan to continue the "Rheinische Zeitung" and its work after an interruption of five years—on the soil of the revolution hoped for five years ago and now become actual. The "Neue Rheinische Zeitung" ap-

---

*The Vendome Column, bearing the statue of the Roman Emperor Trajan. It was a monument of the brutal imperialism of Napoleon the First, and its destruction was decreed on April 12th by the leaders of the Commune.—Translator.

peared. Beside Engels, Wilhelm Wolf—the "casemate wolf," whose name Marx has written on "Capital," Ferdinand Wolf—the "red wolf" who brought along French esprit from Paris; Ernst Dronke, the author of "Secrets of Berlin;" Ferdinand Freiligrath, Georg Weerth, the sensitive poet, brimful of wit—no other paper in Germany has ever had such an editorial staff. The program for Germany was later condensed by Engels in these words: "An indivisible republic and war with Russia including restitution of Poland."

"The 'Neue Rheinische Zeitung,' " writes Engels, "was the only paper within the democratic movement of that time defending the standpoint of the proletariat, as witnessed by its unrestricted championing of the Paris July-insurgents of 1848, whereby it estranged nearly all its stockholders. Vainly the 'Kreuz-Zeitung" (Journal of the Cross) pointed to the 'Chimborazo-impudence' with which the 'Neue Rheinische Zeitung' attacked everything holy, from the king and the administration of the realm down to the policeman, and at that in a Prussian fortress containing a garrison of 8,000 men. Vainly the Rhenish philisterium of Liberals, turned suddenly reactionary, showed a passionate resentment; vainly the martial law in

Cologne suspended the paper during a rather long term in the fall of 1848; vainly the Frankfort Imperial Department of Justice denounced article after article to the state prosecutor for legal prosecution—the paper was calmly edited and printed in plain view of the main guard house, the circulation and the reputation of the journal increased with the violence of the government and bourgeois attacks. When the Prussian coup d' etat followed in November, 1848, the 'Neue Rheinische Zeitung' called on the people at the head of every issue to refuse the taxes and to meet force by force. In the spring of 1849, brought before a jury on account of this and of some other article, it was declared 'not guilty' both times. At last, after the May-revolutions of 1849 in Dresden and in the Rhineland had been suppressed and the Prussian campaign against the uprising in Baden and in the Palatinate was inaugurated by the concentration and mobilization of considerable troops, the government considered itself strong enough to suppress the 'Neue Rheinische Zeitung' by force."

The first number of the "Neue Rheinische Zeitung" appeared on June 1, 1848, the last on May 19, 1849. The last, the "red number," printed on red paper, bears at the head the splendid poem of Freiligrath, who published several of his

most powerful poems in the "Neue Rheinische
Zeitung:"

Kein offener Hieb in ehrlicher Schlacht,
Mich faellten die Nuecken und Tuecken,
Mich faellte die schleichende Niedertracht. * * *

Not by open blow in honest fight,
I'm felled by hook and crook,
By meanness sneaking in the night. * * *

   *   *   *   *   *   *   *   *   *

The revolution had moved in a descending
line since June 1848—since the Paris June-bat-
tle, which had shown to the frightened bourgeoisie that the proletariat had attained its
fighting age.

On November 9, 1848, Robert Blum died on
the Brigittenau in Vienna, pierced by Austrian
bullets directed by martial law, and on the
same 9th of November—nearly at the same
hour—Wrangel entered Berlin and declared the
state of siege. But the revolutionary fire flick-
ered up once more in the spring of 1849, after
the refusal of the king of Prussia and the other
princes to accept the constitution of the realm.
The revolution was confronted by the choice,
either to take up arms for a last effort or to be
slowly crushed by the reaction victorious in
Berlin and Vienna. The time for the pen had

passed momentarily—it was the day of the sword.

While Engels went to Baden and the Palatinate, taking part in the "constitutional campaign," although free from illusions and conscious of its futility, Marx went to Paris where the radical middle class was preparing a "grand action" against the bourgeoisie shying at the red color and eager for a stroke of diplomacy.

This action also miscarried—the radical middle class is nothing without the laborers, and the flower of the laborers had been shot in June, 1848, or had fallen a prey to the "dry guillotine."* The "13th of June," 1849, only revealed the impotency of the radical middle class. Ledru Rollin, the principal hero of the miscarried "action," had to flee to London, as one year previous his colleague, Louis Blanc, had fled after the June battle. And Marx was forbidden by the government to stay in Paris or the rest of France with the exception of the Bretagne which was considered fire-proof. Marx declined the Bretagne offer with thanks and went to London.

And here he remained—after seven years of wandering. Rest, however, did not come to him, nor did he wish for it.

---

*Cayenne, the French convict colony in Guiana, South America.—Translator.

Here in London, the metropolis (mother city) and the center of the world and of the world trade—on the watch-tower of the world whence the trade of the world and the political and economical bustle of the world may be observed in a way impossible in any other part of the globe—here Marx found what he sought and needed: the bricks and the mortar for his work. "Capital" could be created in London only.

In London, Marx and his friends kept aloof from the foolish attempts at re-igniting the ashes and the dross of the February and March revolutions. The coup d' etat of December 2, 1852, for which Marx erected in his "Eighteenth Brumaire of Louis Bonaparte" a monument of shame as immortal as Dante's "terrible tercettes"—destroyed the last prospects of a revolutionary revival. For a while the "Communist Alliance" continued to exist, but after the Communist process in Cologne, ending on the 12th of November, 1852, with the condemnation of the defendants and demonstrating the hopelessness of further propaganda in Germany so far as it could be directed from London, the Communist Alliance was dissolved. Whoever wishes to gain further information about these proceedings may read the "Disclosures about the Communist

Process in Cologne, 1853," written by Marx and republished in a new edition.

An attempt (1850) to continue the publication of the "Neue Rheinische Zeitung" in form of a review—of irregular volumes—from London (via Hamburg), was soon wrecked by the unfavorable conditions.

After the dissolution of the "Communist Alliance," Marx devoted himself entirely to his scientific studies and to journalism. He had become acquainted with David Urquhart, the talented explorer of the Orient and student of the oriental question and Russian politics, and he helped him to reveal and expose on the pillory of newspaper articles and pamphlets the shameful asininities and crooked dealings of the Middle and West European diplomacy, especially of Lord Palmerston. For the "New York Tribune" he wrote as a regular contributor a long series of brilliant articles on political conditions and economic questions—articles containing an invaluable material that should be published also in German translation on account of their contemporary value and as examples of politico-economic writing.

In 1859, the "Critique of Political Economy" was published, demonstrating for the first time Marx's theory of value.

The Italian war of 1859 drew Marx once more into politics. Bonaparte, who for good cash managed for the money-bags the dictatorship of the bourgeoisie, had become the idol of the international bourgeoisie. The German middle class was especially infatuated with him—just as a little later they were with his clumsier imitator, Bismarck, and are at present with Crispi. When he declared war against Austria for the liberation of Italy in order to steady his tottering throne, the emperor of the coup d' etat suddenly became an advocate of democratic ideas; and the Prussian Government which at that time already planned the establishment of a "Greater Prussia" at the expense of Austria, tried to exploit the Bonaparte enthusiasm of the liberal bourgeoisie and to fish in troubled waters. A newspaper founded in London, "The People," to which Marx and his friends contributed, antagonized those lying "attempts at overthrow" and exposed mercilessly the character and aspirations of the French empire.

On this occasion the German ex-regent of the realm, Carl Vogt, who, like other heroes of the "revolution," had secured an appointment at the democratic court of Napoleon and his "red prince," Plonplon, was handled somewhat roughly, thereby drawing forth from him an abusive article swollen with poison and phrases. The abusive article of Vogt was the cause of Marx's classic pamphlet, "Herr Vogt"—aside from its polemical portion, a veritable treasure-box for the students of the contemporary and also of the world's history.

Of course, the liberal bourgeoisie joined Mr. Vogt in abusing like jackdaws Marx and his "sulfur gang" and in accusing him of calumny; but when in 1870 the French Empire collapsed at Sedan, the Tuileries opened their closets— like the famous iron locker that seventy-eight years before furnished the material for the death-warrant of poor Louis XVI.—and from them fluttered forth the papers that demonstrated to all the world the rottenness of the flower of our patriots and professional wise men, among them the receipt for 50,000 francs which "Vogt" had received in August, 1859, immediately after the war, in which he had rendered such good services.

Meanwhile the conditions had become favorable to an independent labor-movement in the different civilized countries. In England, Chartism had become extinct and Trade-Unionism founded on middle-class principles and supporting the middle-class parties no longer satisfied progressive workers. In France, where the awful bloodshed of the June battle was followed by a dreary time of narrow-minded professional organization and philistine consumer's and producer's clubs, the old revolutionary blood began to stir again. And in Germany the workers, roused by Marx's disciple, Lassalle, from their foolish dream of harmony, began to perceive the necessity of class organization and to make attempts at forming an independent political party. Marx now believed the moment had arrived for the organization of an association comprising the labor-movement of the different countries, emphasizing its international conception and rendering possible a common, united action.

On the 28th of April, 1863, a sympathy meeting took place in London for Poland which had just been crushed again by Russia with the help of Prussia. Representatives of the workers of different nations had been invited and it was decided to organize an international workingmen's association. The name, "International Workingmen's Association," was used here for the first time. Three months later, on July 22, a second sympathy meeting for Poland was held in London, in which French laborers especially took part. A thorough debate of the social question took place and the resolution to organize an

"International Workingmen's Association" was renewed. This idea assumed a more definite form, when in the spring of 1864—and again in April—a delegation of workers came from Paris which resolved in a conference with German, Polish, English and American delegates to call an international delegates' meeting for the purpose of founding the "International Workingmen's Association" and to entrust Marx with the preliminary work.

Five months later, on the 28th of September, 1864, in the memorable meeting at St. James' Hall, London, the "International Workingmen's Association" was founded. Marx edited the inaugural address, the program and the constitution of the new organization which was not to be a fighting organization, but rather—so far as was possible under the conditions prevailing on the continent of Europe—a center for all endeavors pointing to the emancipation of the laboring class. The "International Workingmen's Association" was in a certain measure the practical fulfillment of the appeal addressed sixteen years before in the Communist Manifesto to all workers:

PROLETARIANS OF ALL COUNTRIES, UNITE!

The "International Workingmen's Association"

was called a nest of conspirators by the international reaction—but hardly ever was there a political organization so far removed from everything conspiratory. It was a "conspiracy" like the whole labor movement; a conspiracy in broad daylight—public like open nature, public like the history of humanity.

The same battles that Marx had had in the beginning of the London exile with the instigators of revolution who fancied they could revolutionize the world through "energetic will-power" and personal sacrifice, he had to meet in the "International Workingmen's Association." The Willich & Co. reappeared in the Bakunin & Co., who patched together from the wardrobe of the bourgeois hyper-individualism (called hyper-humanity—Uebermenschlichkeit—in Nitzsche's German), a horrible dummy costume that terrified the weak-nerved civilian, but which represented to the initiated only a ridiculous mask of confused backwardness of reasoning.

But this is part of a later time.

In 1867 the first volume of "Capital" appeared—"Critique of Political Economy."

Like all great events, this, too, was not recognized at once in its full importance. Aside from the comrades of the party, the number of those who immediately recognized and acknowledged the value of this work was only small. But they grew irresistibly, and to-day Marx's "Capital" dominates social and political science like Darwin's works in the science of natural history. And there is no thinking proletarian in all the countries of the globe who does not know that this "Capital" is an armory filled with the "mental weapons" that, wielded by the proletariat, will insure its emancipation.

Marx has finished only one volume. Only one. When the lioness of the fable was ridiculed by a cat because she had given birth to one cub only instead of half a dozen, she said proudly: "Only one, but a lion."

The later volumes were not yet finished when Marx died. They have been as far as possible prepared for the press and published by his second self and trusty executor of his testament, Engels.

Three years after the publication of "Capital," in 1870, the Franco-German war broke out as a natural consequence of Bismarck's blood and iron policy and of the "national' disruption of Germany, ridding France of one imperial power and bestowing on Germany another.

Marx viewed the situation with the eyes of the student of history who traces the movements of the political atmosphere and the formation of events, as the meteorologist does the currents of the air, to fixed laws; who does not suppose, but understands; who does not mistake wishes and fancies for facts, but at once separates the actual and vital points from the surrounding misty circle of fantastic conceptions and calculated obscurity.

He fully approved the standpoint and the bearing of the German Social Democracy; and when the dynastic jingoism discarded its mask after Sedan and announced the war of conquest, Marx addressed to the party delegates at Brunswick that letter, published in the "Brunswick Manifesto," penetrating and illuminating as with Roentgen-rays the innermost recesses of things and predicting the consequences of the policy of annexation with a definiteness and accuracy that fill one with awe of this mind capable of computing to a nicety the effects of the factors in question, because he had recognized th ɜm.

Meanwhile the terrible war of brothers raged on, sowing hate among two nations whose friendship means the peace of the world and whose enmity means a constant threat of war.

The French laborers, who, like the German laborers, had protested against the war and, not content with this, had destroyed the imperial sovereignty after Sedan, were in favor of a revolutionary conduct of the war by a general call to arms and of mobilizing the entire fighting strength of the country, as soon as the German defensive war changed into a war of conquest. They, the "men without a fatherland," defended Paris, which the well-fed "patriots" wanted to deliver to the Germans at once. They defended the republic which had been treasonably abandoned by Thiers and his "patriotic" colleagues, and after France had groveled at the feet of the victorious Germans from fear of an armament of the whole laboring class, they rose on the 18th of March, 1871, for the salvation of the republic.

The commune came on, and to the "International Workingmen's Association" fell the task—not of directing, for this was out of the question from the first, but of carrying on or rather of helping to carry on a hopeless yet necessary struggle against the enemies of the republic and of the laboring class in as good a manner as was possible under the circumstances.

The commune was suppressed by superior force and the "International Workingmen's Association," the terror of the civilized world, was outlawed in all countries.

What the commune was, what its struggle and

death signified, is told by "The Civil War in
France," written by Marx with his own life-
blood and that of the commune, of which he
was a part as the founder of the "International
Workingmen's Association."

*   *   *   *   *   *   *   *   *

The "International Workingmen's Association" found itself in an entirely changed position
after the downfall of the commune. The field
of practical action was cut off for the time being and those sectarian differences and utopian
conspiracies mentioned a while ago found a
favorable soil.

Marx, who in his office of General Secretary,
was crowded more and more by work and re-
sponsibility and who above all owed it to himself and to the party to finish his "Capital,"
was forced to bring about a change. After making short work of the Bakunin bow-wow an-
archism in a crushing critique ("The alleged
schisms in the International Workingmen's Association"), he suggested the transfer of the
headquarters of the association to New York,
and at the congress of the Hague in 1873 a resolution to that effect was passed.

Whatever may be thought of this resolution
that has been variously criticized, Marx was enabled by it again to devote himself with full

force to his scientific work and to advance the "Capital" so far, that the work as a whole could be completed in its fundamental outlines, the second volume almost entirely and the third in some important parts.

Although the work accumulated under his hands more and more, yet Marx followed with live interest the labor movement in all countries, especially in Germany. His letter on the outline of a program for the congress of union at Gotha (1875) was recently recalled to the memory of the comrades by the proceedings of the party—meeting in Halle and Erfurt (1890 and 1891). Although the interests of the party forbade an immediate acceptation of Marx's propositions for fear of wrecking the chances of union, yet they have received full recognition at the revision of the party program since the abolition of the socialist laws and have been of potent influence for the new ("Erfurt") program.

Sickness, brought on by excessively hard work, undermined Marx's originally very strong constitution and forced him in the seventies to go to Karlsbad and the south of France. Family misfortunes overwhelmed him. Death reaped his harvest. On the second of December, 1881, his Jenny died—the playmate of his youth, his comrade for life, his friend, his adviser, his fellow-fighter. This blow struck him through the heart. With her he himself died. Her death was his death. We who knew him felt this well.

A voyage to Algiers and the south of France did not bring him more strength. I was appalled when I saw him again in the summer of 1882. He did not complain—the deadliest blows kill the nerve, they do not cause any pain—only death. He did not recover. And then came the finishing stroke: Little Jenny, his favorite daughter, the image of himself, Longuet's wife, died suddenly after a short illness. He remained apprehensively calm on receiving the news. In the winter of 1882-3 he was attacked by pneumonia which, however, seemed to take a favorable course. It was even believed that he was convalescent. Vain hope.

On the 14th of March he died quietly in his armchair, with hardly a struggle.

His daughter concludes her sketch of his life with Shakspeare's immortal words for an epitaph:

* * * "the elements
So mixed in him that Nature might stand up
And say to all the world: 'This was a man.' "

What Antonius says of Brutus who, vanquished, died at the point of his own sword—this is true in still greater measure of Marx, the un-vanquished and invincible in the battle of minds and of spirits:

"This was a man"   *   *   *

And Engels wrote to me:

"London, March 14, 1883.

"Dear Liebknecht:

"My telegram to Mrs. B——, the only address I have, will have informed you what a fearful loss the European socialist revolutionary party has experienced. Only last Friday the phy-sician—one of the most prominent in London—had told us that there was a good chance to make him as healthy as he had ever been be-fore, if we could only hold his strength by nourishment. And just from that time on he recommenced to eat with more appetite. Sud-denly at two o'clock this afternoon I found the house in tears, because he was frightfully weak. Lenchen called me upstairs; he was half asleep, and when I came up he was wrapped wholly in sleep—but eternally. The greatest mind of the second half of our century had ceased to think. About the real cause of his death I do not permit myself to make any state-ment, without the advice of a physician, and the whole case was so intricate that it would require whole sheets to have it described even by doctors. But this is really of no more con-sequence now. I have suffered a great deal of anxiety during the last six weeks, and I can only say that in my opinion, first, the death of his wife, and then, at a very critical point, that of Jenny have done their share to bring about the final crisis.

"Although I have seen him to-night stretched out on his bed, the face rigid in death, I cannot grasp the thought that this genius should have ceased to fertilize with his powerful thoughts the proletarian movement of both worlds. Whatever we all are, we are through him; and whatever the movement of to-day is, it is through his theoretical and practical work; without him we should still be stuck in the mire of confusion. Yours,   F. ENGELS."

    *   *   *   *   *   *   *   *   *

It is not the scope of this work to determine and estimate the scientific importance of Marx. Neither can it be my intention to reveal here the fundamental outlines of his politico-economic doctrine. That has been done in publications known and accessible to all comrades. Only about one point I wish to make a short statement; about the so-called "materialistic conception of history" that is so frequently mentioned of late years both appropriately and inappropriately.

Of the materialistic conception of history, which, though not "discovered" by Marx as Engels expresses it, yet has been for the first time clearly defined and applied with methodic consciousness by him, Engels writes:

"The first of the important discoveries with which the name of Marx is associated in the history of science, is his conception of the world's history. 'All conception of history previous to him is founded on the idea that the ultimate causes of all historic changes are found in the changing ideas of men, and again that of all historic changes the political are the most important, controlling the whole of history. But whence these ideas are derived by men, and what are the moving causes of political changes nobody had ever inquired. Only in the recent school of French and partly also of English historians, the conviction had forced itself that at least since the Middle Ages the driving force in European history was the struggle of the developing bourgeoisie with the feudal nobility for the social and political supremacy. Marx, however, demonstrated that all history has been hitherto a history of class-struggles, that all the numerous and intricate political struggles were carried on only for the sake of the social and political supremacy of different classes in society; for the maintenance of the supremacy by older, for the establishment of supremacy by newly rising classes.

"Through what agency, now, do these classes rise and exist? Through the pressure of those material and physical conditions under which the society of a given time produces and exchanges its means of subsistence. The feudal reign of the Middle Ages was based on the self-sufficient and almost exchangeless management of small farming communities, producing nearly all their own necessities and receiving from the warlike nobility protection against external foes and national, or at least political, coherence. When the towns arose and with them a separate branch of skilled industry and a trade first confined to the home market, but later on waxing international, then the civic element of the towns developed and, fighting the nobility, obtained even during the Middle Ages its admission as a likewise privileged class into the feudal order. But by the discovery of new lands outside of Europe in the middle of the fifteenth century, the bourgeoisie obtained a far more extended territory for its trade and hence a new incentive to industry; skilled labor was displaced in the most important branches by more factory-like production which in its turn met the same fate through industrial organization on a large scale made possible by the inventions of the last century, especially the steam-engine. These industries reacted on trade by displacing manual labor in the more backward countries and creating in the further advanced countries the present new means of communication, steam-engines, railroads, electric telegraphs. Thus the bourgeoisie united more and more the social wealth and the social power in its own hands, though for a long time it still remained excluded from the political power which still rested in the hands of the nobility, and the monarchy protected by the nobility. But at a certain stage—in France after the great revolution—it also conquered this power and now became in its turn the ruling class in opposition to the proletariat and the small farmer. Observed from this point of view, all historical transactions are very easily explained—with a sufficient knowledge of the contemporaneous economic state of society, unhappily wholly missing in our professional historians; and in a most simple manner the conceptions and ideas of a given historical period are explained by the economic conditions of existence during that period, and by the social and political conditions dependent on those economic factors. History for the first time was placed on its real foundation; the obvious fact, hitherto totally neglected, that first of all men must eat, drink, have shelter and clothing, and therefore must work, before they can struggle for supremacy and devote themselves to politics, religion, philosophy, etc.—this obvious fact at last found historical recognition."

Thus writes Engels in his biographic sketch of Marx from which I have repeatedly quoted. The word, "class-struggles," is used by him in its widest sense, in the sense of struggles of interests based on contemporary conditions of production. That these struggles will assume a different form in a nomadic nation than in a nation of hunters, and in an agricultural nation a form different from that in an industrial nation— this is without any further explanation just as self-evident as the fact that the German empire could not have been founded by a nation of

Dahomey negroes. The German empire—it is always well to choose your examples from your closest surroundings—offers an admirable illustration for the correctness of the materialistic conception of history. The German bourgeoisie that applauded the thought of an empire and sees to this day the essence of the most brilliant diplomatic wisdom in Bismarck's blood and iron policy was, fifty years ago, from the first to the last man liberal, democratic, hated militarism, ridiculed the police rule—in short, opposed everything it venerates or at least deems necessary to-day.

What explains this change? The German bourgeoisie has become capitalistic.

As long as industrial production on a small scale predominated, the bourgeois element, oppressed and subjected to petty violence by the feudal-bureaucratic government, had an interest in opposing the administration and in coveting the political power—thus it was "democratic."

Ever since the bourgeoisie has become capitalistic, that is, since production on a large scale prevailed, and on one hand the class-antagonism brought to a climax, forced the proletariat into the class-struggle under the banner of Socialism, while on the other hand production on a small scale was ruined by competition—henceforth that part of the bourgeoisie not forced into the proletariat is itself a ruling class whose dominating and living issue is the utilization of the existing means of government for its service and the alliance with such elements of a backward civilization controlling the government as clergy, feudal nobility and so forth. In this manner the Democratic German bourgeoisie has become "Bismarckian" and imperialistic under our very eyes—solely in consequence of the evolution of local production on a small scale to capitalistic production on a large scale.

And again this evolution, like all former progress of industry, culture and politics, is the natural consequence of the endeavor founded in human nature continually to improve our conditions of existence. And more favorable conditions of life mean improved tools, increased productiveness of labor.

Thus human civilization is the work and product of the tools of labor.

It is true, "the history of Man is the history of his tools"—of his tools and of the forms of production dependent on the tools.

MEMOIRS.

How I became acquainted with Marx, I re-lated more than a year ago in a little sketch for Fuchs' "Volksfeuilleton," "A bad quarter of an hour." There I wrote:

"The friendship—with Marx's two eldest daughters, then 6 and 7 years old—began a few days after I had come to London from Switzer-land, forcibly transported through France from a jail of 'free Switzerland.' I found the family of Marx at a summer picnic of the Communist Laborers' Educational Club, somewhere near London, I don't remember whether in Green-wich or in Hampton Court. 'Pere Marx,' whom I saw for the first time, began at once to sub-ject me to a rigid examination, looked straight into my eyes and inspected my head rather min-utely--an operation to which I was accustomed through my friend Gustav Struve, who, ob-stinately doubting my "moral hold," had made me the specially favored victim of his phreno-logical studies. However, I safely passed the examination, sustaining the look of that lion-head, with the coal-black lion's mane; the ex-amination became a vivacious, merrily rippling

chat, and soon we were in the middle of the
merry-making—Marx one of the most exuber-
ant—where I at once became acquainted with
Mrs. Marx, with Lenchen, from her youth their
faithful household assistant, and with the children. Some other time, when I have more leisure, I shall relate more of Marx's family—it is a
debt of gratitude of which I must acquit myself,
and also a duty towards my comrades who have
a right to demand that every one who can contribute to the completion of the picture of the
only Marx and his surroundings should do so
to the best of his power. Enough—from that day
on I was at home with Marx, and I never missed
a day in his family then living in Dean street, a
court running off Oxford street, while I made
my quarters in neighboring Church street. Of
Marx I shall not speak here. His wife has
perhaps exerted as strong an influence on my
development as he did himself. My mother died
when I was 3 years old; and I was brought up
somewhat hard. I was not accustomed to earnest intercourse with women. And here I found
a beautiful, noble-minded, high-spirited woman
who in a half sisterly, half motherly way, took
care of the friendless fighter for liberty, driven
ashore on the banks of the Thames. The intercourse with this family—I am fully convinced—

has saved me from succumbing to the misery of the exile."

* * * * * * * * *

My first lengthy conversation with Marx took place the day after our meeting at the aforesaid picnic of the Communist Laborers' Educational Club. There, of course, was no opportunity for a satisfactory exchange of opinions, and Marx had invited me to the clubroom for the following day, where I should probably also meet Engels. I arrived a little before the fixed time; Marx was not yet there, but I found several old acquaintances and was engaged in animated conversation, when Marx, saluting me very warmly, patted me on the shoulder and invited me downstairs to Engels in the private parlor, where we should be left more to ourselves. I did not know what a private parlor was, and I had a presentiment that now the "main" examination was impending, but I followed confidingly. Marx, who had made the same sympathetic impression on me as the day previous, had the quality of inspiring confidence. He took my arm and led me into the private parlor; that is to say, the private room of the host—or was it a hostess?—where Engels, who had already provided himself with a pewter-pot full of dark-brown stout, at once received me with merry jokes. In a trice we had ordered Amy (or Emma, as the refugees had re-baptized her in German, on account of the similarity of sound), the sprightly waitress (I soon formed a better acquaintance with her; she married one of my comrades of Becker's corps), in a trice we had ordered "stuff" to drink and to eat—with us fugitives the stomach question played a paramount part—in a trice the beer had been brought and we seated ourselves, myself on one side of the table, Marx and Engels opposite me. The massive mahogany table, the shining pewter-pots, the foaming stout, the prospect of a genuine English beefsteak with accessories, the long clay pipes inviting to a smoke—it was really comfortable and vividly recalled a certain picture in the English illustrations of "Boz." But an examination it was for all that! Well, let it come. The conversation waxed more and more fluent. I soon found that my examiners had already gathered information concerning me. A lengthy composition on the June battle I had written for Hecker's "Volksfreund" in Muttenz in the summer of 1848 under the fresh impressions of the tragedy that marked a new historical era, had been read by Marx and Engels and had attracted their attention to me. I had not entertained any personal relations to them previous to meeting Engels in Geneva the year before. Of Marx I had only known the articles in the Paris annals and the "Poverty of Philosophy," and of Engels the "Condition of the Working Classes in England." The "Communist Manifesto" I—a communist since 1846—had been able to obtain only shortly before my meeting with Engels after the constitutional campaign, although I had heard of it before, of course, and knew the contents; and the "Neue Rheinische Zeitung" I had seen very rarely, indeed. During the eleven months of its publication I had been either abroad or in prison or in the chaotic storm and strife of life in the free-corps.

I was suspected by both my examiners of philistine "Democracy" and "South German sentimental haziness." And many a judgment I pronounced on men and things met with a very sharp criticism. Nevertheless I succeeded in clearing myself of that suspicion. I had only to relate how I had fared in Baden with the citizen "Democracy," how Brentano, after the second disturbance (the "Struve fizzle"), had declined, after a violent controversy, to defend me before the jury that had summoned me for high treason and other crimes, because I had refused to deny my communist faith; how the

same Brentano two months later in the middle
of the outbreak, had sent me to the casemates
of Rastatt on the charge of having planned an
assault on him, and how subsequently he had
been sharply criticized by his friend Hecker,
because he did not have me shot summarily be-
for a court martial.

On the whole, the examination did not take an
unfavorable course, and the conversation slowly assumed a wider scope. Soon we were on
the field of Natural Science, and Marx ridiculed
the victorious reaction in Europe that fancied it
had smothered the revolution and did not suspect that Natural Science was preparing a new
revolution. That King Steam who had revolu-
tionized the world in the last century had ceased
to rule, and that into his place a far greater
revolutionist would step, the electric spark. And
now Marx, all flushed and excited, told me that
during the last few days the model of an electric
engine drawing a railroad train was on exhibi-
tion in Regent street. "Now the problem is
solved—the consequences are indefinable. In
the wake of the economic revolution the political must necessarily follow, for the latter is
only the expression of the former." In the way
that Marx discussed this progress of science and
mechanics, his conception of the world and

especially that part later on called the materialistic conception of history became so clearly
apparent that certain doubts I had hitherto entertained vanished like snow in the sun of
spring. That evening I did not get home—we
talked and laughed and drank till late the next
morning, and the sun was already up when I
went to bed. And I did not stay in bed long.
I could not sleep. My head was too full of
everything I had heard; the thoughts, surging
to and fro, drove me out again, and I hastened
to Regent street in order to see the model, this
modern Trojan horse that civilized society, like
the Trojan men and women of old, was leading
jubilantly into its Ilios in suicidal blindness,
and that would surely bring on its destruction.
Essetai haemar—the day will come when the
ɩoly Ilios will fall.

A great crowd indicated the show-window be-
ʌind which the model was exhibited. I forced
my way through; to be sure, there was the engine and the train, and engine and train were
spinning around merrily.

It was then 1850, the beginning of July. And
to-day it is 1896, the beginning of April. Forty-
five years and a half have passed, and no railroad train is yet driven by an electric engine.
The few street cars and whatever else is oper-

ated by electricity do not signify much on the whole, however much it may appear. And in spite of all revolutionizing inventions it will take some time yet before lightning, completely tamed, will allow itself to be hitched to the yoke of human labor and will drive King Steam from his throne. Revolutions are not accomplished in a sleight-of-hand fashion. Only the sensational shows in politics are called revolutions by the wonder-working rustic faith. And whoever prophesies revolutions is always mistaken in the date.

Well, though Marx was a prophet looking into the future with sharp eyes and perceiving much more than ordinary human beings, he never was a prophesier, and when Messieurs Kinkel, Ledru Rollin and other revolution-makers announced in every appeal to their folks in partibus the typical, "To-morrow it will start," none was so merciless with his satire as Marx.

Only on the subject of "industrial crises" he fell a victim to the prophesying imp, and in consequence was subjected to our hearty derision which made him grimly mad. However, in the main point he was right none the less. The prophesied industrial crises did come—only not at the fixed time. And the causes of the prolonged intervals have been demonstrated by Marx with scientific perfection.

Apropos of this subject, let me mention that the verse against the prophets of revolutions in the famous poem of Freiligrath to Weidemeyer was inspired nearly literally by Marx while we were sitting together one evening with the "Tyrtaios of the Neue Rheinische Zeitung," who had a very susceptible ear for available remarks and generally conveyed them immediately to his notebook.

The enormous power and vital strength of civilized society has been recognized by none so well as by Marx. And England is just the right place for such a revelation. Here human society has developed most purely, one may say truly classically, and without casting aside all forms still in the concrete has overcome and excreted most thoroughly all the rubbish of previous centuries and social forms.

A would-be diplomat, Mr. von Bennigsen, has lately launched in the German Reichstag the wise saying that the army is the strongest pillar of civilized society. If that man had been in England or had only an inkling of English conditions, he would not have committed himself to such a barrack-room pun. England has no army and society there stands on a foundation of such strong material and composition that the "rocher de bronce"* of militarism in comparison to it is worm-eaten, mouldering junk. On the contrary, this "rocher de bronce," with its middle age absolutist plunder that breeds in it is a mill-stone around the neck of human society, hindering it in swimming and drawing it down to the bottom, while unweighted it would have strength to keep above water for a long time yet. The nervousness of the German bourgeoisie looking, like Prince Bismarck, to Dr. Eisenbart for salvation and regarding as its last remedy soldiers, policemen, and "si duo faciunt idem non est idem"*-jurists, is an unmistakable sign that in Germany society has no longer any faith in itself. And when in its desperation it increases the weight by which it is drawn into the abyss, it imitates the senseless exertions of a drowning man who by these same exertions removes the last chances of rescue and accelerates the catastrophe.

* * * * * * * * *

After relating how I became acquainted with Marx, let me also relate at the same time how I did not become acquainted with him—that is, how I missed making his acquaintance when

---

*Bronze rock.
*If two are doing the same thing, it is not the same. This is the principle of class legislation.—Translator.

the iron broom of revolution had swept me quite close to him.

By a hair's breadth I should have met Marx in February, 1848, immediately after the February bluster We were only a few hundred paces distant from each other without my being aware of it. I had hastened from Switzerland—from Zurich—to Paris on hearing the news about the outbreak of the street-fight in Paris; by Julius Froebel I was recommended to Herwegh, to whom I betook myself at once. "The iron lark" was busy fitting out the German legion, and as the thought of carrying the republic from France to Germany appeared beautiful as well as feasible to my not quite 22-year-old brain, I was easily won for the adventure. While I crawled on the birdlime, a more circumspect man who could look also behind the scenes was busily engaged in preventing the nonsense. For he understood that the plan of organizing "foreign legions" for the purpose of carrying the revolution into other countries emanated from the French bourgeois-republicans, and that the "movement" had been artificially inspired with the twofold intention of getting rid of troublesome elements and of carrying off the foreign laborers whose competition made itself doubly felt during this grave business crisis. This other man was Marx, of whose presence I did not learn in the whirl of excitement. And if I had learned of it, Herwegh would have done his utmost to keep us apart. Enough, I did not meet Marx—otherwise he would have carried me along in his wake then and there without a doubt. I should not have come to South Germany, but probably to Rhenish Prussia and perhaps into the office of the "Neue Rheinische Zeitung." Well, it was not so to be. And we did not meet until two years later.

And still another man I did not meet in Paris at that time, one whom I could not meet later on. And him I did not meet, although I knew that he was in Paris. I mean Heinrich Heine. I admired his poems, but the two facts that he received a pension from Louis Philippe and contributed to the "Augsburger Allgemeine Zeitung," were in my eyes, still looking through the colored glasses of social revolutionary romanticism, such capital crimes that I could not arrive at the decision to visit the "hireling of reaction." How I have suffered from remorse in after days! But it was a lost opportunity that did not return. And the irony of fate decreed that later on I should myself become a correspondent of the "Augsburger Allgemeine Zeitung."

EDUCATIONAL AND OTHER NOTES— MARX AS TEACHER.

Marx endeavored to make sure of his men and to secure them for himself. He was not such a zealous devotee of phrenology as Gustav Struve, but he believed in it to some extent, and when I first met him—I have already mentioned it—he not only examined me with questions, but also with his fingers, making them dance over my skull in a connoisseur's style. Later on he arranged for a regular investigation by the phrenologist of the party, the good old painter, Karl Pfaender, one of the "oldest," who helped to found the Communist Alliance, and was present in that memorable council to whom the Communist Manifesto was submitted, and by whom it was discussed and accepted in due form. On this occasion a comical incident happened. One of the "old ones" of the Communist Laborers' Educational Club was very enthusiastic over the manifesto that was read by Marx with passionate emotion—perhaps similarly as the "Robbers" once upon a time by Schiller—was quite beyond himself, like all others, applauded and shouted "Bravo!" as loud as he could; but his pensive mien gave evidence that some dark point occupied his mind. On leaving he finally called Pfaender aside: "That was magnificent, but one word I did not understand—what does Marx mean by 'Achtblaettler' (plant with eight leaves)?" "Achtblaettler, Achtblaettler—I have heard of plants, of clover, with four leaves, but 'Achtblaettler?' " Pfaender was puzzled. At last the riddle was solved. Marx had a little lisp in his youth and at that time still spoke the unadulterated Rhenish dialect; the mysterious 'Achtblaettler,' behind which the old Cabetist had scented a magic formula, were simple and honest—Arbeiter (workingmen). We laughed many a time over this misunderstanding which, however, was beneficial to Marx in that henceforth he strove to clip the wings of his Rhenish dialect.

Well, my skull was officially inspected by Karl Pfaender and nothing was found that would have prevented my admission into the Holiest of Holies of the Communist Alliance. But the examinations did not cease. "Mohr," who in possession of his start of five or six years was conscious of the full superiority of ripe manhood over us "young fellows," used every opportunity to test us, and especially me. And with his colossal scope of reading and his fabulous memory he could make it rather unpleasant for us. How he rejoiced when he had tempted a "little student" to go on the ice and demonstrated on the person of the unfortunate the inadequateness of our universities and of academic culture.

But he educated, too, systematically. I can say of him for two reasons, in the more limited and in the wider sense of the word: he was my teacher. And one had to follow him to all fields of knowledge. Political economy I need not mention. In the palace of the Pope it is superfluous to speak of the Pope. Of the lectures on Political economy in the Communist Club I shall speak later on. In the ancient and modern languages Marx was equally well at home. I was a philologist, and it gave him a childlike pleasure when he could show me some difficult passage from Aristotle or Aeschylos in which I could not at once find my way. How he scolded me one day because I did not know any—Spanish. Quickly he snatched up Don Quixote from a pile of books and gave me a lesson without loss of time. From Dietz' "Comparative Grammar of the Romanic Languages" I knew the fundamental outlines of grammar and etymology, and so we went along smoothly under "Mohr's" excellent guidance and his careful help, when I stumbled or paused. And how patient he was in teaching, he who otherwise was so stormily impatient! Our lesson was brought to a close only by the entrance of a visitor. And every day I was examined and had to translate from Don Quixote or some other Spanish book—until the proof of my capability seemed sufficiently established.

Marx was an excellent philologist—true, more of modern than of ancient languages. The German grammar of Grimm he knew to a nicety, and in the German dictionary of the brothers Grimm, so far as it had been published, he was better versed than I, the philologist. He wrote English and French like an Englishman or a Frenchman, though he had some difficulty in pronouncing. His articles for the "New York Tribune" are written in classic English; his "Misere de la Philosophie" against Proudhon's "Philosophie de la Misere" is written in classic French—the French friend who revised the manuscript for him before it went to press found very little to correct.

Marx, being familiar with the spirit of languages and having occupied himself with their origin, development and organism, found no difficulty in learning languages. In London, he was still learning Russian, and during the Crimean war he even had the intention of learning Arabic and Turkish which, however, was abandoned. Like every one who really wishes to master a language, he attributed the principal value to reading. Whoever has a good memory—and Marx had a rare memory that never relaxed its hold—will easily acquire possession of the treasures of word and expression by much reading. Their practical use is then easily learned.

* * * * * * * * *

During the years 1850 and 1851 Marx delivered a course of lectures on Political Economy. He made up his mind to it rather unwillingly; but once he had read a few private lectures to a small circle of friends, he yielded to us and agreed to teach before a larger audience. In this course that was a rare treat to all who had the good fortune to take part in it, Marx already developed his system in all its fundamental outlines, as presented to us in "Capital." In the crowded room of the Communist Alliance, or "Communist Laborers' Educational Club," at that time still domiciled in Great Windmill street—in the same room where one year and a half previous the Communist Manifesto had been confirmed—Marx exhibited a remarkable talent of popularizing. Nobody hated more than he the vulgarizing of science, that is the

adulterating and rendering it shallow and spirit-
less; but nobody possessed in a higher degree
the quality of expressing himself clearly. Clear-
ness of speech is the fruit of clear reasoning, a
clear thought necessitates a clear form.

Marx proceeded methodically. He stated a
proposition—the shorter the better, and then
demonstrated it in a lengthier explanation, en-
deavoring with utmost care to avoid all expressions incomprehensible to the laborers. Then he
requested his audience to question him. If this
was not done he commenced to examine them,
and he did this with such pedagogic skill that
no flaw, no misunderstanding, escaped him. I
learned on expressing my surprise about his dexterity that Marx had formerly given lectures on
political economy in the laborers' club in Brussels. At all events he had the qualities of a
good teacher. He also made use of a black-
board, on which he wrote the formulas—among
them those familiar to all of us from the beginning of "Capital."

What a pity that the course lasted only about
six months or even less. There were certain elements entering the Communist Alliance that did
not suit Marx. After the waves of the flood
of fugitives had subsided the Alliance shrunk
together and assumed a somewhat sectarian

character—the old Weitlingians and Cabetists resumed their pompous ways and Marx, whom such a narrow sphere of action did not satisfy, and who could do something better than sweep away old cobwebs, kept aloof from the Communist Alliance. For my part, I did not follow his example, but considered it my duty to keep in touch with the only German labor organization in London. I had been a member of the German Laborers' Club in Zurich as far back as 1847-48, and however little I had been of benefit to the club—a knave gives more than he has —I had profited a great deal myself. And thus I also regarded the London Communist Alliance in the light of a Laborers' Educational Club— such was its rightful name—for myself. I felt that I had much to learn which I could learn only by intercourse with laborers, and though I would fain have had a wider sphere of motion and action I still was content with the small one in the absence of a larger. And I have never regretted it. With the exception of one year when I was prevented by political differences I have been a regular member of the Communist Alliance up to the day of my departure from London, have given lectures there and lessons in German, English, French and other studies.

The club was even the cause of a conflict

with Marx. However high he stood to me and however much I loved him, infallibility was not recognized, and if I did not find in debate that I was wrong I did not admit of being overruled by another's opinion. Marx himself was, of course, within the confines of communistic conceptions, the most tolerant of men. He could stand opposition, although not unfrequently he flew into a passion over it; and afterwards he even enjoyed having received a strong answer. But by men who were more "Marxian" than Marx himself—who did not wish to be called a "Marxist" and ridiculed the "Marxists" to his heart's content—plots were woven against me, and one fine day I found myself charged with the crime of violating our principles by my actions in the London Communist Allance, of having made concessions to the Weitlingian and other sectarians that were inadmissible from a tactical and theoretical standpoint, of trying to gain an unorthodox counterbalance against the orthodoxy of the Communist Alliance, and to have deviated from the straight road through the attempt of playing the role of a "mediator" between the pure communistic doctrine and the practice, especially between Marx and the workingmen. The spirits met in a lively clash. Marx violently deprecated the "mediator business;"

if he had anything to say to the laborers he
could say it himself. This I did not deny, of
course, but I maintained my right to serve the
party in a way that seemed most appropriate
to me, and declared it crazy tactics for a workingmen's party to seclude itself away up above
the workers in a theoretic air-castle; without
workingmen, no workingmen's party, and the
laborers we must take as we find them. You
see, it was a conflict that has been repeated
later on. By personal instigations this trifling
incident was inflated to a conflict, and I remained in the minority. This embittered me; and for
several months I eschewed the house of Marx.
But one day the children met me on the street;
they scolded me for staying away so long; their
mamma, they said, was quite mad with me,
and—I went along with them, was received as
usual, and Marx himself, whose originally serious look melted when I stepped close to him,
laughingly shook my hand. And that conflict
was mentioned no more.

Disputations I have had by the score with
Marx—a quarrel with him only twice. This
was the first time. The second was some twenty years later, and, curiously enough, over the
same subject. It was in 1874: the longing for
unity between the Lassallians and the "honest

ones" made itself equally felt on both sides
and the political conditions made union a necessity. But there were still certain prejudices
to respect, and in the program for union out-
lined by ourselves we had to submit to certain
concessions. Marx, who could not survey the
conditions of things from abroad as well as we
in Germany, would not hear of such concessions;
and after a prolonged exchange of opinions
with me that famous letter was written about
which so much was said some years ago.
Marx was highly incensed against me for a
long time, but in the interest of the movement
in Germany I had had no other choice. If
it had been a question of sacrificing a principle,
Marx certainly would have been right; but it
was only a matter of yielding temporarily for
the purpose of securing great tactical advan-
tages for the party. And it cannot be called a
sacrifice of principle when the sacrifice is made
in the interest of principle. That I did not
make a wrong calculation in this respect has
been brilliantly demonstrated by the consequences and the successes. The declaration of
principles was accomplished within the united
parties so speedily and so smoothly that, had
not the "law of exception" during the time of
its validity forced the program-question into

the background, we could have proceeded with the clarification of the program as early as the close of the seventies without any opposition worth mentioning. As it was, this had to be postponed to the beginning of the nineties.

Marx has finally acknowledged this. He was charmed by the progress of the party-movement in Germany, and shortly before his death he said to me: "I am proud of the German laborers: without a doubt they are leading the international labor movement." Similarly Engels has expressed himself, although he retained his animosity on account of the program for union for a longer time.

Marx was no orator—it was not his nature. In the Hague, at the last congress of the International Workingmen's Association, he is said to have spoken very well, so I have been told. I was at that time with Bebel in the "fortress" Hubertusburg. I have never heard him making a speech; neither was there any opportunity for him during the time of our association.

* * * * * * * * *

It is claimed that Marx had no "style"—or at least a very bad style. This is claimed by those who have no idea of style—polishers of words and twisters of phrases who have not understood and were not capable of understanding

Marx—not capable of following the flight of his genius to the highest peaks of science and passion and into the lowest depths of human misery and human baseness. If ever Buffon's word was true of any man it was in regard to Marx: The style is the man—the style of Marx is Marx. A man so thoroughly true who knew no other cult but that of truth, who in a moment would cast aside dearly acquired and cherished propositions whenever he had convinced himself of their inaccuracy, could not but show his true self in his writings. Incapable of hypocrisy, incapable of acting and posing, he was always himself in his writings as in his life. True, in a nature so manifold, so far embracing, so multiform, the style cannot be so uniform or evenly balanced or even simple as in less complex, less embracing natures. The Marx of "Capital," the Marx of the "Eighteenth Brumaire" and the Marx of "Mr. Vogt" are three different Marx's—and in their differences still the one Marx—in their trinity still a unit—the unit of a great personality expressing itself differently on different topics and still remaining the same person. Certainly the style of "Capital" is difficult to understand—but is the subject it treats of easy to grasp? The style is not only the man, it is also the subject-matter

—and it must be adapted to the latter. "There is no royal road to science"—everyone has to exert himself and to climb, even with the best of guides. To complain of the difficult, obscure or clumsy style of "Capital" is only revealing one's own slothfulness of thought or incapability of reasoning.

Is the "Eighteenth Brumaire" unintelligible? Is the dart incomprehensible that flies straight at his target and pierces the flesh? Is the spear unintelligible that, hurled by a steady hand, penetrates the heart of the enemy? The words of the "Brumaire" are darts, are spears—they are a style that stigmatizes, kills. If hate, if scorn, if burning love of freedom ever found expression in flaming, annihilating, elevating words, then it is surely in the "Eighteenth Brumaire," in which the aroused seriousness of Tacitus is united to the deadly satire of Juvenal and the holy wrath of Dante. The style is here what it—the stylus—originally was in the hands of the Romans—a sharp-pointed steel pencil for writing and for stabbing. The style is the dagger used for a well-aimed thrust at the heart.

And in "Mr. Vogt"—this laughing humor—this joy suggestive of Shakespeare finding a Fal-

staff and with him an inexhaustible mine from
which to fill an armory with sarcasm!

Let us waste no more time discussing the style
of Marx. Marx's style is just Marx. For trying to squeeze into the smallest possible space
the greatest possible contents he has been
blamed, but that is just Marx.

Marx atached great value to a pure, correct
expression. And in Goethe, Lessing, Shakespeare, Dante, Cervantes, that he read almost
daily, he had chosen the great masters. In regard to purity and precision of language, he was
of painstaking conscientiousness. I remember
well that once during the first time of my stay
in London he gave me a severe lecture because
I had said in an article: "die stattgehabte Ver-
sammlung" (the meeting held). I tried to ex-
cuse myself with the colloquial use of the language, but Marx broke out: "Those miserable
German colleges where one cannot learn any
German, those miserable German universities"
and so forth. I defended myself as best I could,
I cited also examples from classic authors, but—
I have not spoken any more of a "stattgehab-
ten" or "stattgefundenen" occurrence, and I
have prevailed on many others to discard it. On
the other hand I saved, in that battle about the
intransitive past participle, the "gelernten

Schuster" (shoemaker by trade) by the help of the "gelehrten Schuster" (learned shoemaker) whom Marx could not well recognize as correct.

Marx was a rigid purist—he often searched tediously and long for the right expression. He hated the superfluous foreign words, and while he nevertheless has made frequent use of foreign words—where the subject did not make them imperative—it is necessary to take into consideration his long stay in foreign countries, especially in England—and, a very essential reason, the affinity of German and English, rendering mistaken substitutions easy. In "Capital" Marx is speaking, e. g., of "zusammengehudelten Menschen" (people huddled together) where he was thinking of the English "huddle together", that has nothing in common with our "hudeln" (to praise fawningly), except the first origin, and means "to squeeze together, to intermingle without order." But what an infinite wealth of original, genuinely German forms and applications of words do we find in Marx, who, although he passed two-thirds of his life in foreign countries, deserves great credit for his advancement of the German language and is one of the most distinguished masters and creators of the German language.

He was a purist, sometimes to the extent of

becoming pedantic. And my Upper-Hessian dialect, that obstinately clung to me—or I to it—was the cause of innumerable censures. In these skirmishes I was lucky to have an ally whom Marx respected as highly as I did myself. I mean my Hessian countryman—although not born in officially so-called Hesse—the Frankforter, Wolfgang Goethe. I used the forms: hunten, unten, drunten (below, under), hoben, oben, droben (up, above), haussen, aussen, draussen (out, outside),hueben, ueben, drueben (beyond, over there), and so forth. This always aroused Marx, who had a strong antipathy against the "hunten, hoben, haussen," but finally decided on Goethe's authority to tolerate, if not to indorse them By telling such trifling incidents I wish to show how Marx felt his place as a teacher in relation to us "young ones."

This naturally expressed itself in many other ways. He demanded much. No sooner had he discovered a flaw in our knowledge than he urged impetuously that it be remedied—he offering the necessary advice. On being alone with him you had to submit to a regular examination. And these examinations were no joke. Marx was not to be hoodwinked. And when he found that nothing would avail, it was all over with

his friendship. It was an honor for us to be dis-
ciplined by him. Never was I with him without
learning something. And that I did not go to
the bottom in the hard struggle for existence,
for the naked physical life, or let us rather
say for keeping from starving—because we had
to hunger for years in London—that I did not
perish in this desperate struggle for a piece of
bread or a few potatoes, I owe to Marx and his
family.

* * * * * * * * *

On account of my affection for Marx I was
often ridiculed by friends and comrades of a
time prior to my stay in London. Only lately
I found a letter written by one of the most
active Badish members of the free-corps, by
Bauer of Sinsheim, who died a few years ago
in Milwaukee as the editor of a radical democratic newspaper established by himself. After
a short stay in London he had gone, like most
of the fugitives possessing the necessary means,
to the United States, where he soon had found a
congenial occupation in the newspaper business.
It was during the worst time of the London exile, and he wanted me to join him at all events.
In several letters he had already invited me,
offering me the certain prospect of a considerable editor's salary. And when you have not

even dry crusts to whet your teeth, then $50 per
week, which he had offered me, is quite an
alluring bait. But I withstood; I did not wish
to depart any further than necessary from the
battlefield, and whoever goes "across" to the
other side of the great water is lost to Europe
in 999 cases out of a thousand. Finally Bauer
tried his best trump: he flattered my self-love.
In a letter which I still have among my papers
he wrote: "Here, then, you are a free man—you
can independently accomplish something. And
over yonder? A play-ball—an ass serving as
packmule and afterwards ridiculed. How do
you get along in your heavenly realm?   Up
above is enthroned the Omniscient, the All-
Wise, your Dalai Lama Marx. Then follows a
great, great void.   And then comes Engels.
And then comes another great, great void. And
then comes Wolf. And then again comes another great, great void. And then, perhaps,
comes that "sentimental ass" Liebknecht. Well,
I answered that I had no objection to coming
after men who had accomplished more than I—
that I preferred to be in the society of men from
whom I could learn and to whom I could look
up rather than of such on whom I should have
to look down, as would be the case with all his
"great men."

And I staid where I was,—and learned.

But such was the judgment pronounced on
Marx and our society by the fugitives outside of
our circle; that we secluded ourselves completely
from them, stimulated their fancy and produced
a maze of myths and gossip, which, however,
did not turn our hair gray.

*   *   *   *   *   *   *   *   *

POPULARITY.

For popularity Marx entertained a sovereign
contempt. What he especially praised in Robert Owen was that whenever any of his ideas
became popular he would come forth with a
new demand making him unpopular. Free from
all conceit, Marx could not attribute any value
to the applause of the masses. The masses
were to him a brainless crowd whose thoughts
and feelings were furnished by the ruling class.
And while Socialism has not spiritually soaked
through the masses, the applause of the crowd
can, as a logical consequence, be bestowed only
on men belonging to no party or to the adversaries of Socialism. To-day, when socialistic
conceptions have begun to pervade the masses
and to influence so-called "public opinion," this
is no longer true to the same extent as 40 or
50 years ago. Then it was only a tiny minority
within the laboring class itself that had raised

itself to Socialism; and among Socialists themselves those in the scientific sense of Marx— in the sense of the Communist Manifesto—were in the minority. The bulk of the laborers, so far as they had become awake to political life, were wrapped in the mists of sentimental democratic wishes and phrases, such as were a part of the movement of 1848 with its preludes and epilogues. The applause of the masses: popularity—was to Marx a proof of being in the wrong and his favorite quotation was the proud verse of Dante:

Segui il tuo corso e lascia dir le genti.

(Follow your course and let the people talk.)

How often has he quoted this verse that also concludes his preface to "Capital." Nobody is impervious to blows, thrusts, stings of mosquitoes or bugs, and how often may Marx, following his course, attacked on all sides, worried by cares of existence, misunderstood by the mass of the workingmen for whose battle of freedom he was forging the weapons in the stillness of the night, even scorningly disavowed by them while they were running after shallow phrasetwisters, glistening traitors or, perhaps, open enemies—how often may he, in the solitude of his poor, genuinely proletarian study, have cheered his own courage with the words of the great

Florentine and gathered new strength from
them!

He was not to be turned aside from his purpose. Unlike the prince in "Arabian Nights,"
who lost the victory and the price of victory
because he was tempted by the noise and the
phantasms around him to look timidly around
and backward, he proceeded in his path, his
eyes steadily directed ahead at the shining goal
—he "let the people talk," and if the world's orb
had crumbled to pieces nothing would have
restrained him in his course. And victory came
to him. True, not the price of victory.

Before all-conquering Death felled him he
had lived to see the seed he had scattered growing up wonderfully and ripening for the scythe of
the harvester. Yes, he had the victory—and we
have the price of victory.

Popularity being hateful to him, he felt a holy
wrath against soliciting popularity. Smooth-
tongued orators were an abomination to him,
and woe to him who indulged in phrases There
he was inexorable. "Phrase-monger" was in
his mouth the sharpest censure—and whomever
he once had recognized as a "phrase monger"
he ignored forever. To think logically and to
express your thoughts clearly—this he impress-

ed on us "young fellows" on every occasion and forced us to study.

About this time the magnificent reading-room of the British Museum, with its inexhaustible treasures of books, had been built—and thither, where he passed a certain time every day, Marx drove us. To learn! To learn! This was the categorical Imperative he frequently enough loudly shouted to us, but it also was expressed by his example, yea, by the sole aspect of this forever strenuously working mind.

While the rest of the fugitives were laying plans for the overthrow of the world and in-toxicating themselves day by day, evening by evening with the hasheesh-drink of: "To-morrow it will start!"—we, the "sulphur-gang" the "bandits," the "scum of humanity," were sitting in the British Museum and trying to educate ourselves and to prepare arms and am-munition for the battles of the future.

Sometimes we would not have had a bite, but that would not prevent our going to the Museum—there were at least comfortable chairs to sit down on and in winter a cheering warmth —which were missing at home, if one had any "house" or "home" at all.

* * * * * * * * *

Marx was a strict teacher; he did not alone

urge us to learn, but also convinced himself whether we did learn or not. I had given some time to studying the history of the English trade unions; every day he asked me how far I had progressed, and finally he did not rest till I had given a longer lecture to a large audience. He was present. He did not praise me, but neither did he assail me with criticisms, and since praising was not his custom and he generally praised only from pity, I consoled myself about the missing praise; and when after that he entered into a disputation with me over an assertion I had made I regarded it as indirect praise.

Marx as a teacher had the rare quality of being strict without discouraging.

And still another excellent teacher's quality had Marx: he forced us to criticise ourselves and he did not countenance a satisfaction with the attained. He cruelly whipped the easy-going flesh of contemplation with the scourge of his satire. And none had to thank him more for this training than I. Youth rejoices in the success of the moment and in applause. I have never been fond of speaking. Even in a circle of friends I am not very talkative. The resolution to make a speech has always cost me a little self-compulsion; and even to this day, unless Duty demands it categorically, I prefer to let

others speak instead of speaking myself; but I
should lie were I to deny that the enthusiastic
acclamations of a meeting numbering thousands
whom I am holding as by hypnotic power and
filling with my thoughts, with my feelings—that
this magnetic power over a roaring sea of human beings has something wonderfully intox-
icating. However, I have never forgotten the
dangers of popularity; and if I remain unmoved
by applause and praise—as unmoved as by the
abusive language and the calumnies of our enemies— it is an art I have learned from Marx,
although it necessitated the school of a life full
of struggles to hammer it into me.

* * * * * * * * *

Politics was to Marx a study.   Beer-politi-
cians and barroom politics he viewed with deadly hate.   And, indeed,is anything more devoid of
sense conceivable?   History is the product of all
the forces active in Man and Nature and of human thought, of human passions, of human
wants.   But politics is, theoretically, the recognition of these millions and billions of factors
busy at the "loom of Time," and, practically,
action based on this recognition.   Politics is
also science and applied science; and political
science or science of politics is, as it were, the
essence of all science, for it embraces the whole

field of action of Man and Nature, which action is the goal of all science. Nevertheless every ass thinks himself a great politician or even a great statesman—as every ass thinks himself a good newspaper editor. For both purposes—according to common belief—it is unnecessary to have learned anything; one is "born" for them, to quote Professor Sohm of Leipsic.

How wild Marx could become when speaking of those hollow skulls who arrange matters for themselves with a few cant phrases and, mistaking their more or less confused wishes and ideas for facts, direct the fate of the world at the beer-table, in newspapers or in public meetings and parliaments Happily, the world does not take any notice of them. By those "hollow skulls," very famous, highly celebrated "great men" were sometimes meant.

In this point Marx has not simply criticised, but he has also given a standard example, and especially in his writings on the later development of France and on the coup d'etat of Napoleon, and furthermore in his letters to the N. Y. Tribune he has furnished classic examples of political representation of history.

Here a comparison suggests itself to me. Napoleon's coup d'etat, treated by Marx in his "Eighteenth Brumaire," was also made the subject of a famous publication by Victor Hugo, the greatest French romancer and phrase-juggler. What a contrast between the two publications and the two men! There the monstre-phrase and the phrase-monstre, here the facts, methodically arranged—the coolly meditating man of science and the politician, wrathful, but never losing his serene judgment through his wrath.

There fleeting, resplendent spray. Eruptions of pathetic rhetoric, grotesque caricatures—here every word a well-aimed dart, every sentence a weighty charge loaded with facts, the naked truth, overwhelming in its nakedness—no indignation, only demonstration, fixing of that which is. Victor Hugo's "Napoleon le Petit"—Napoleon the Little—had ten rapidly following editions and is to-day forgotten. And Marx's "Eighteenth Brumaire" will be read admiringly after thousands of years. Victor Hugo's "Napoleon the Little" was a lampoon—Marx's "Eighteenth Brumaire" is a historic work that will be to the economic historian of the future—and the future will not know any other but economic history—just as indispensable as to us the history of the Peloponnesian War by Thucydides.

*   *   *   *   *   *   *   *   *

Marx—I have mentioned it before it in another place—could become what he was only in England. In a country economically so undeveloped as Germany was up to the middle of this century Marx could no more arrive at his Critique of Polititical Economy and at the recognition of the capitalistic mode of production than this economically undeveloped Germany could have the political institutions of economically developed England. Marx was dependent on his environment and the conditions under which he lived as much as any other man; and without this environment and without these conditions he would not have become what he did. Nobody has demonstrated this better than himself.

To observe such a mind while it is subjected to the effects of the conditions surrounding it and penetrating deeper and deeper into the nature of society—that in itself is a great intellectual treat, and I can never praise my good luck sufficiently for leading me, a young, inexperienced lad, thirsting for knowledge, to Marx and bringing me under his influence and his teaching.

And considering the manifold, yea, one might say all-embracing, accomplishments of this widely informed genius — this mind encircling the universe, penetrating into all the essential details, considering nothing below his attention as being unimportant and trifling—the tutelage necessarily had to be universal.

Marx was one of the first to comprehend the importance of Darwin's investigations. Even before 1859, the year of the publication of the "Origin of Species"—by a singular coincidence also the year of the publication of Marx's "Critique of Political Economy"—Marx had recognized the epochal importance of Darwin, who, far from the noise and stir of the great cities, in his peaceful country home, was preparing a revolution similar to the one Marx was initiating himself at the turbulent centre of the world—only that he inserted his lever at a different place.

Especially on the field of natural science—including physics and chemistry—and of history Marx closely followed every new appearance, verified every progress; and Moleschott, Liebig, Huxley—whose "Popular Lectures" we attended conscientiously—were names mentioned in our circle as often as Ricardo, Adam Smith, Mc-Culloch and the Scotch and Irish economists. And when Darwin drew the consequences of his investigations and presented them to the public we spoke for months of nothing else but Darwin and the revolutionizing power of his scientific conquests. I emphasize this, because "radical" enemies have spread the idea that Marx, from a certain jealousy, acknowledged the merit of Darwin very reluctantly and in a very limited degree.

Marx was the most generous and just of men, when it came to acknowledging the merits of others. For envy and jealousy as well as for conceit, he was too great. Only the false greatness, the artificial fame inflated by incompetence and vulgarity, he regarded with a deadly hatred —as he did everything false and adulterated.

*   *   *   *   *   *   *   *   *

MASKS, MEN AND PHOTOGRAPHS.

Marx was one of the few among the great, little and average men known to me who was not vain. He was too great for it and too strong—and, may be, too proud. He never posed and was always himself. Like a child he was unable to carry a mask and to simulate. Except where caution was required for social or political reasons, he always lent word to his thoughts and feelings completely and frankly, and expressed them in his face. And when restraint was necessary, he showed an almost childlike lack of dexterity that often amused his friends. He had no diplomatic ability, although or rather because he was a great politician. The greatest commonwealth, the United States of North America, has no displomats, and barbaric Russia has the best ones.

Never was there a more truthful man than Marx—he was Truth personified. By looking at him one knew at once what to expect. In our "civilized" society with its permanent state of war one cannot, of course, always speak the truth—that would be equivalent to delivering yourself into the hands of the enemy or inviting social ostracism—but though it may not always be feasible to tell the truth, still it is not necessary to utter falsehoods. I cannot always reveal what I think and feel, but that does not imply a necessity or a compulsion to say what I do not feel and think. The one is good sense, the other, hypocrisy. And Marx has never played the hypocrite. He simply was incapable of doing it—just like an unspoiled child. And his wife has often called him "my big child." Nobody has known and understood him better than she—not even Engels. And really, when he went into society—save the mark—where attention was paid to external forms and where restraint was required, our "Mohr" was like a little child indeed and would become bashful and red like a little child.

Posing people were an abomination to him. I

remember how he laughingly related to us his first meeting with Louis Blanc. It was still in Dean street, in the little lodging that in truth consisted of two rooms only, of which the front room, the parlor, served as reception room and study, while the back room served for everything else. Louis Blanc had been received by Lenchen who led him into the front room, while Marx quickly dressed himself in the back room; but the door connecting the two rooms had been left open, and the chink revealed to him a ludicrous spectacle. The great historian and politician was a very small manikin, not higher than a boy eight years old, but terribly vain withal. After looking around awhile in the proletarian salon he had discovered in some corner the extremely primitive mirror, before which he at once took his place, struck a pose, stretched his dwarfed frame to the utmost—he had the highest heels on his boots I ever saw—"salaamed" like an amorous rabbit in March, contemplating himself affectionately, and studied the most imposing attitude attainable. Mrs. Marx, who was also a witness of this comical scene, could hardly refrain from laughing. When Marx had finished his toilette, he announced his entry by clearing his throat noisily, enabling the coxcomb of a popular tribune to retreat a step from the mirror and receive his entering host with a stylish bow. Nothing, however, could be accomplished with Marx by posing and acting. And in consequence "Little Louis"—as the Parisian laborers called him in contradistinction to Louis Bonaparte—soon behaved as naturally as he still was capable of doing.

It has been said that all men are actors. This is not true. But the majority of civilized ones are so without a doubt, and I have always divided the people into actors and non-actors. The great majority belongs to the first class. When I am at leisure, I amuse myself on the street and on the train by observing people and studying the contrast between those who show their true selves, and those who play a part. And how few are there who do not play a part— I refer here only to educated people. Among servant girls and laborers of both sexes many natural faces are to be found—not so among the educated higher classes. There almost every one has his or her mask. In order to see that most people are actors, no tedious physiognomic studies are required—one has only to look at their photographs. The sun does not lie. And yet, how few photographs are likenesses. Why? Because he or she who is photographed wishes to appear as beautiful, as good, as daring as interesting, as brilliant, as thoughtful and deep, as enterprising, as full of strength as possible, as gifted with everything imaginable. In short, he and she are acting. He and she put on their ideal mask. And not their true self, but their mask is brought out by the honest, truthful sun. The sun does not deceive. But the people who are photographed by him, deceive themselves and their fellow-beings. And deceive so well that often one cannot recognize them at all.

The study of photographs is, therefore, extremely instructive; and though the person may deceive, and though the photograph may deceive, there cannot be any deception when we have the person and the photograph before us.

Of Marx I know no bad photographs. They are all good likenesses, because he has always given himself as he was. True, the photographs have not all the same value. The characteristic lines of a person's face do not always show equally well—bodily or mental uneasiness or disease, the domination of a certain thought or sensation may give a strange character to a face. But all photographs of Marx are good.

"GENIUS IS DILIGENCE"

Has been said by some one, and though this

may not be entirely true, it is so at least to a great extent.

No genius without extraordinary working power and extraordinary amount of work. The so-called genius lacking these two is only a glittering soap-bubble or a time-draft on treasures in the moon. But wherever working power and amount of work above the average are found, there is also genius. I have met many men who were mistaken by themselves and also by others for geniuses, but who possessed no working power—and they were only loafers with much suasion and talent for advertising themselves. All really great men whom I have known were very diligent and worked hard. In Marx this was the case to the highest degree. He worked tremendously hard; and being very often hindered during the day time—especially in the first period of the exile—he took refuge in the night. When we went home from some meeting or session, he would sit down regularly and work for a few hours. And these few hours extended more and more, until finally he worked nearly all night and slept in the morning. His wife reasoned with him earnestly—but he said laughingly that it suited his nature. I had become accustomed myself during my college time to executing the more difficult exercises late in the evening or during the night, when I felt mentally most active, and did not, therefore, view the matter from the same standpoint as Mrs. Marx. But she was right. And in spite of his extremely strong constitution, Marx began to complain of all kinds of disorders in his bodily function, at the end of the fifties. The advice of a physician had to be obtained. A peremptory order forbidding all night work was the result. And much exercise, that is bodily exercise: long walks, long rides were prescribed. During this time I wandered about frequently with Marx in the country surrounding London, especially in the hilly north. He soon recovered—for indeed, he had a body admirably adapted to great exertions and great disiplay of strength. But hardly did he feel well, when he gradually relapsed into the habit of working at night, until another crisis occurred, forcing him to adopt a sensible mode of living—but always only as long as necessity made itself imperatively felt. The crises became more violent—a liver complaint developed and virulent ulcerations appeared. And gradually that iron constitution was undermined. I am convinced—and this is also the verdict of the physicians who treated him last—that Marx, if he could have prevailed on himself to lead a natural life, that is a life corresponding to the requirements of his body or, let us say, of hygiene, might be alive to this day. Not until the last years—when it was too late—did he give up night work, and he then worked all the more during the day time. He always worked whenever it was any way feasible. Even on his walks he carried his note-book and made entries from time to time. And his work was never superficial. There is work and work. He always worked intensely, thoroughly. From his daughter Eleanor I have received a historical table he had devised for the purpose of gaining a general view of some trifling footnote. But nothing was trifling to Marx, and this table for his momentary private use is arranged with as much diligence and care, as if it had been intended for publication.

Marx worked with an endurance that often filled me with wonder. Fatigue was unknown to him. He had to break down—and even then he did not manifest any languor.

If the value of men is computed according to the work they have accomplished—as the value of products by the amount of labor they represent—then Marx, from this point of view alone, is of such a high value that only a few of the mental giants can be placed at his side.

And what has human society given in ex‹ change for this enormous sum of work?

On "Capital" he was at work forty years—and how he did work! Only a Marx can work so. And I am not exaggerating when I say: the worst paid day laborer in Germany has received more wages in forty years than Marx did for a salary, as an honorary fee for one of the two greatest scientific creations of this century. The other one is represented by Darwin's works.

"Science" is not a market value. And can we expect that human society would pay a decent price for the execution of its own death warrant?

* * * * * * * * *

FRIEND AND TEACHER.—URQUHART.

Were I to sketch even the most hasty outlines, I should not find time and space to present here all those persons I have met during that period in the house of and in company with Marx. Besides those German and other fugitives who were not separated from us by political enmity, the leaders of the English labor movement— Julian Harney, the Spartan character, Ernest Jones, the eloquent tribune of the people and fiery journalist, the last two great standard bearers of Chartism that was absorbed by Social- ism—Frost, who condemned to deportation for

life as the leader of the Chartist revolt returned
to England in the fifties after being pardoned:
the most conspicuous of the "physical force
men"—; and Robert Owen, the aged patriarch of
Socialism, by far the most embracing, penetrating and practical of all the harbingers of scientific Socialism. We were present at the meeting celebrating his eightieth birthday, and I had
the good luck to associate with him personally
on frequent occasions in his home.

An extremely interesting acquaintance was
that with David Urquhart, the best expert on
Russian diplomacy and Turkish conditions.
Through Urquhart, to whose most zealous ad-
herents and disciples Lothar Bucher, then still
advocating a "Greater Germany," belonged, we
were cured from the romantic ideas, spread by
Byron and the "Hellenic Songs" of Wilhelm
Mueller in regard to "Homer's people" and to
other Christian nations of Turkey in the civilized countries and especially in Germany, according to which every Greek was a hero and
every Turk a perjured, cruel scoundrel. We
found out that this was partly legend, partly
lie. David Urquhart, who had lived for many
years in Turkey, had traveled through the country in all directions and had entertained, as a
member of the British Embassy in Constanti-

nople, and still was entertaining intimate relations to many "statesmen" and diplomats "at
the source"—was perfectly informed on everything relating and belonging to the "Oriental
question," an authority of the first order, yea,
the highest authority. A surprising knowledge
of men and things, added to genuine Scotch
penetration, gave weight to every word of
Urquhart. Genial, tenacious, a diplomatic de-
tective, he followed Russian politics on all its
crooked trails, to all its mole-tunnels, and
watched step for step his mortal enemy, Lord
Palmerston, whom he regarded—and truly not
without good reason—as the conscious tool of
Russia. Whoever wishes to learn more about
Urquhart may read about him in the letters of
Bucher to the "National Zeitung." The hatred
against Parliamentarism imbibed by Bucher in
England is due principally to David Urquhart,
who demonstrates in his writings a hundred
times that Lord Palmerston was enabled by
parliamentary corruption to play the game of
absolutist Russia and at the same time to
enact the role of the popular despot-hater and
revolutionary "firebrand" of Europe. The hate
against parliamentarism became destructive for
the grim hater of Russians, Lothar Bucher—it
made him an easy prey of the cynical connoisseur

of men, Bismarck, although the latter was "more Russian than the Russians" and—in spite of all differences—a sort of German Palmerston.

Marx convinced himself of the correctness of Urquhart's judgment and views, and he advocated them—especially during the Crimean war—with burning zeal and with his characteristic strength in the press and in pamphlets. We were connected with Urquhart up to the time of his death, and I must also pay him my little tribute of gratitude in these pages, for whatever I may have been able to contribute in party papers, in pamphlets and in the Reichstag to illustrating the incapacity of our professional diplomatists and to stigmatizing the Russian policy of conquest and corruption, I owe in the first place to my intercourse with Urquhart and to Urquhart's writings.

Russian diplomacy has not changed and at the present time, when the disastrous war of brothers between Germany and France has brought to the Russian barbaric diplomacy the office of arbitrator, I can recommend the study of Urquhart's writings ("Portfolio," "Progress of Russia," etc.) most earnestly. The enthusiastic advocates of "Bismarck's great foreign policy" will then discover how this "great" and also "national" policy was dictated by Russian diplomatists and directed by them on puppet-strings.

BARTHELEMY.

A short while after my arrival, a Parisian laborer came to London, in whom not only the French colony was deeply interested, but all of us fugitives as well, and most likely also our "shadow": the international police. It was Barthelemy, about whose escape from the Conciergerie, accomplished by him with admirable adroitness and daring, we had heard already through the papers. A little above medium height, powerful, muscular, coal-black curly hair, piercing black eyes, the image of determination—a splendid specimen of the type of Southern Frenchman. A wreath of legends surrounded his proudly erect head. He was a "galerien"—a galley-convict—and had on his shoulder the indelible brand. When a 17-year-old "gamin," he had killed a police sergeant during the Blanqui-Barbes revolt in 1838, and had been sentenced to the Bagno for it. The February revolution brought him an amnesty—he returned to Paris, took part in all the movements and demonstrations of the proletariat, and fought in the June battle. On one of the last barricades he was caught and happily not recognized by anybody during the first days—

otherwise he would have been shot, no doubt,
"summarily," like so many others. When he
was brought before the court martial, the first
rage had subsided, and he was condemned to
the "dry guillotine," viz: to transportation to Cayenne for life. The process had been delayed—
I don't know for what reason—enough, in June,
1850, Barthelemy was still confined in the Conciergerie, and immediately before his departure
to the land where the pepper grows and men die
he effected his escape, of course, to London.
Here he entered into closer relations with us
and was frequently in Marx's house. Mrs.
Marx did not like him—he was uncanny to her,
his piercing eyes were repulsive to her. I
fenced frequently with him—I mean in reality.
The Frenchmen had opened a "fencing salon"
in Rathbone Place, on Oxford street, where
fencing with sabres, swords and foils and pistol-
shooting could be practiced Marx also came
now and then and lustily gave battle to the
Frenchmen. What he lacked in science, he
tried to make up in aggressiveness. And unless you were cool, he could really startle you.
The sabre is used by the Frenchmen not alone
for cutting, but also for thrusting, and that in-
conveniences a German a little at first. But
one soon becomes accustomed to it. Barthelemy

was a good fencer and practiced pistol-shooting frequently, thereby becoming an excellent marksman in a short while. He drifted into the company of Willich and there contracted a spite against Marx. Marx was a "traitre," because he would not conspire and disturb the peace—we heard such phrases often enough later on,— and "the 'traitres' must be killed." I tried to reason with him—but in vain.

The differences with the Willich sect grew bitter, and one evening Marx was challenged by Willich. Marx had the proper contempt for these Prussian officers' frolics, but the young comrade Schramm, a hotspur, now insulted Willich on his part, thus forcing the latter to challenge him according to his own code of honor. It was agreed to fight the duel in Belgium on the sea coast with pistols. Schramm had never had a pistol in his hand previous to the challenge, while Willich never missed the ace of hearts at twenty paces. He took Barthelemy as a second. We were alarmed for the life of our fresh, chivalrous Schramm. The day fixed for the duel passed on—we counted the minutes.

In the evening of the following day the door of Marx's house is opened—he was not at home, only Mrs. Marx and Lenchen—and enter Barthelemy bowing stiffly and replying with a

sepulchral voice to the anxious question "What
news?" "Schramm a une balle dans la tete!"—
Schramm has a bullet in his head—whereupon
bowing stiffly once more he turned and with-
drew. You may imagine the fright of the half
insensible lady; she knew now that her instinc-
tive dislike had not deceived her.

One hour later she related the sad news to us.
Of course, we gave up Schramm for lost. The
next day, while we were just talking about him
sadly, the door is opened and in comes with a
bandaged head but gaily laughing the sadly
mourned one and relates that he had received a
glancing shot which had stunned him,—when he
recovered consciousness, he was alone on the
sea coast with his second and his physician.
Willich and Barthelemy had returned from Os-
tende on the steamer which they had just been
able to reach. With the next boat, Schramm
followed.

Barthelemy found a tragic end. He conceived the plan to kill Napoleon. In order to
be sure, he intended to shoot him not with a
bullet, but with deer shot steeped in sulphur,
and in case that should miscarry to stab him.
He had obtained an admission card for the next
ball at the Tuileries which Napoleon would be
sure to visit. Money and everything else he

had—but after the French fashion also a "lady friend" whom he wished to take with him. On the way to the boat he remembers that he— he was a very skilled mechanic—has a debt outstanding with his last "patron" (boss). Being in the neighborhood he wishes to get the money. He enters—the "lady friend" waits at the door— there, suddenly a dispute, a report—people gather about, policemen hurry to the house, enter it—the proprietor is lying on the floor in his last throes. Where is the murderer? The house has also an exit through the yard. And then another shot is heard, and still another,— one policeman lies in his blood, another, though wounded, holds Barthelemy until help arrives.

The mystery about the occurrences in the house was soon cleared. Barthelemy asks for his money, the proprietor directs him to his office, Barthelemy becomes violent, the proprietor threatens to throw him out, thereupon Barthelemy who feels that he is the weaker man sees "blood," draws his rovolver—fires and kills; he wishes to save himself, in front the people are already assembled—he runs through the back door intending to jump over the back wall into an adjoining street—in the meantime two policemen have also arrived there. He kills one and wounds the other (Dec. 3, 1854).

It was a sensational trial that excited all England. Was it murder or manslaughter? The jurists were unanimous that it was the latter, for according to English law murder requires premeditation. But it was clear that Barthelemy did not think of murdering when he entered the house, he had been attacked and acted in self-defense, although beyond discretion. And just as surely there was no premeditation on firing the other two shots. Therefore he could have been sentenced only for manslaughter under aggravating circumstances to a long imprisonment.

But Barthelemy was sentenced to death and hanged. How was that possible?

The "lady friend" who—also after the French fashion—had relations with the police was not initiated in the plot, but she had heard this and that and gave information to the police that led to the right trail.

However that may be—to everybody's astonishment the charge was "murder"; the jury, secretly informed of the circumstances, found Barthelemy guilty (Jan. 4, 1855) and he was sentenced and executed (Jan. 22, 1855). This was in 1855—in the honey-moon of the Anglo-French alliance. The London papers of that time contain long pages full of reports on all phases of this trial, that has been thoroughly discussed by Lothar Bucher in his letters to the "National Zeitung."

Later, on visiting Newgate prison, in front of which the execution had taken place, with a friend from Germany, I saw among the plaster-casts of the faces of the hanged men that of Barthelemy, with the impression of the rope clearly visible. The expression was changed very little—the face still showed an iron determination.

* * * * * * * * *

MARX AND THE CHILDREN.

Marx, like all strong and healthy natures, had an unusual affection for children. He was not only the most loving of fathers, who could be a child among children for hours—he also was attracted as by magnetism toward strange children, particularly helpless children in misery that chanced to cross his way. Time and again he would suddenly tear himself away from us on wandering through districts of poverty in order to stroke the hair of some child in rags sitting on a doorway or to slip a penny or half-penny into its little hand. He mistrusted beggars, for in London begging has become a regu-lar trade—and one that still has a golden bottom though collecting nothing but copper. By male or female beggars, therefore, he was not deceived long, although in the beginning—whenever he could afford it—he never refused to give. Against some of them who had taxed him by dint of artful display of artificial disease and suffering, he even had quite a strong spite, because he regarded the exploitation of human sympathy as a particularly flagrant meanness and as a stealing from poverty. But when a beggar or a beggar woman with a whimpering child accosted Marx, then he was lost without fail, though roguery might be written ever so plainly on the forehead of the beggar or the woman. He could not withstand the imploring eyes of the child.

Physical weakness and helplessness always vividly excited his pity and sympathy. A man beating his wife—and wife-beating was then quite the fashion in London—he could have ordered with greatest relish to be beaten to death. By his impulsive character on such occasions he not unfrequently brought himself and us into a "fix." One day I was riding to Hampstead Road with him on the driver's seat of an omnibus, when we noticed at a stopping place in front of a gin palace a crowd from the middle of which a piercing female voice was shouting "Murder! Murder!" Quick as a flash Marx had

jumped down and I after him. I tried to hold
him back—I might as well have tried to catch a
flying bullet with my hands. In a trice we were
in the middle of the crowd; and the human
waves closed behind us. "What is up?" Only
too soon it became evident what was up. A
drunken woman had gotten into a row with
her husband, the latter wanted to take her
home, she resisted and holloed like mad. So
far so good. There was no need of any intervention on our part—we could see that. But
the quarrelling pair saw it also, and making
peace at once attacked us, while the crowd
closed more and more around us and assumed a
threatening attitude against the "damned foreigners." Especially the woman went full of
rage for Marx and concentrated her efforts on
his magnificent shining black beard. I endeavored to soothe the storm—in vain. Had not two
strong constables made their appearance in
time, we should have had to pay dearly for our
philanthropic attempt at intervention. We
were glad when we were out of it without a
scratch and safely seated on another omnibus
that brought us home. Later Marx was a little more cautious with similar attempts at intervention.

* * * * * * * * *

It is necessary to have seen Marx with his children in order to fully understand the deep mind and childlike heart of this hero of science. In his spare minutes or on his walks he carried them around, played with them the wildest, merriest games—in short, was a child among children. On Hampstead Heath we would sometimes play "cavalry": I would take one little daughter on my shoulder, Marx the other one, and then we would jump and trot, outdoing one another,—now and then there would also be a little cavalry engagement. For the girls were wild as boys and could also stand a bump without crying.

For Marx, the society of children was a necessity—he recovered and refreshed himself thereby. And when his own children were grown up or dead, his grandchildren took their place. Little Jenny who married Longuet, one of the fugitives of the commune, in the beginning of the seventies, brought into the house of Marx several boys—wild fellows. Especially the elder, Jean or Johnny, now on the point of "serving" his time in France as an "unvoluntary" volunteer, was grandpa's pet. He could do whatever he pleased with him, and he knew it. One day, while I was on a visit to London, Johnny, whom his parents had sent across from

Paris—as used to be done several times every
year—conceived the ingenious thought to trans-
form "Mohr" into an omnibus on the driver's
seat of which, that is Mohr's shoulders, he seated himself, while Engels and myself were ap-
pointed omnibus horses. And after we had
been duly hitched up, there was a wild chase—
I meant to say a wild drive in the small house
garden behind Marx's cottage in Maitland Park
Road. But perhaps it was in Engels' house on
Regent's Park. The London model homes resemble each other like twins, and the house
gardens more so. A few square yards of
gravel and grass—both thickly covered by a
layer of London black, or "black snow": that
is, the all-pervading soot, in such a manner that
it is impossible to tell where the grass begins
and the gravel ceases—that is the London
"garden."

Then it was "Get up!" with international
German, French and English exclamations—
Go on! Plus vite! (Quicker!) Hurrah! And
Marx had to trot, until the sweat poured down
from his forehead, and when Engels or I would
try to slacken our speed, down came the whip
of the cruel driver: You naughty horse! En
avant! (Go ahead!) And so forth, until Marx
could not stand it any longer,— and then we be-

gan to negotiate with Johnny and a truce was established.

* * * * * * * * *

It was pathetic and at the same time often comical how Marx, who in political and economical discussions did not eschew the strongest, yea most cynical expressions and phrases, would express himself in the presence of children and women with a gentleness that an English governess might have envied. When the conversation then took an ambiguous turn, he became nervously excited, shifted about on his chair, ill at ease and could color like a girl six years old. We young fugitives were a wild set and we delighted among other things in singing worldly songs of a strong calibre; thus it happened one day that one of us who had quite a fine voice, a distinction I cannot claim for any of us others—politicians and especially communists and socialists seem to live in strained relations with the muse of music—began to sing the beautiful but not exactly chaste song of "Jung, jung Zimmergesell" (Young, young carpenter lad). Mrs. Marx was not at home—otherwise we should not have dared it—and nothing was to be seen of Lenchen and the children, therefore we believed we were "by ourselves." Suddenly Marx, who at first had also sung or rather shouted, became restless, and at the same time I heard in the adjoining room a noise indicating the presence of somebody; Marx, who evidently had also heard this noise, shifted about on his chair, the picture of highest embarrassment, until he suddenly jumped up and whispered or hissed with his face glowing red: "Hush! hush! The girls!"

The girls were really so young then that the "young, young carpenter lad" would not have been able to endanger their morality. We smiled a little—he stuttered that it would not be right to sing such songs in the hearing of children. And the "young, young carpenter lad" like other similar songs was not sung any more by us in the house of Marx.

In such matters, by the way, Mrs. Marx was even more sensitive than he. She had a look that made a word freeze to your tongue, if you showed a sign of boldness.

Mrs. Marx exercised, perhaps, a still greater power over us than Marx himself. "This dignity, this loftiness," that kept aloof not familiarity but everything unbecoming, acted with magic power on us wild or even a little rude fellows. I remember with what terror she once filled the "red Wolff"—not to be confounded with the "casemate Wolff" lupus. The former, who had adopted Parisian manners and was very shortsighted, noticed one evening on the street a graceful female figure that he followed. Although he encircled the veiled lady several times, she took no notice of him until he, becoming bolder, came so close to her face that he could distinguish her features in spite of his shortsightedness and—"Hol' mich der Deuwel (may the devil get me)—it was Mrs. Marx!" he related to me excitedly next morning. "Well, what did she say to you?" "Nothing at all, that is the devil of it!" "And what did you do? Did you apologize?" "Hol' mich der Deuwel—I ran away." "But you must apologize! The affair is not so very important!"

But "Hol' mich der Deuwel"—the red Wolff who enjoyed a certain reputation on account of his imperturbable cynicism could not be induced for six months to enter the house of Marx, although I could tell him on the next day that Mrs. Marx, when I sounded her carefully, had broken out in merry laughter at the recollection of the inexpressibly bewildered and frightened face of the red Wolff thwarted in his role as Don Juan.

Mrs. Marx was the first woman who made me recognize the educational strength and power of women. My mother died so early that I

have retained only shadowy, confused conceptions of her; and later on—except a very short
time in my earliest childhood—I also found myself altogether excluded from female company
that might have elevated me and contributed
to the softening and polishing of my nature.
Before meeting Mrs. Marx, I had not understood the truth of Goethe's word:

Willst Du genau erfahren was sich ziemt,
So frage nur bei edlen Frauen an!
(If thou wouldst know exactly what is meet,
Go, ask of noble women what they think!)

She was to me now Iphigenia softening and
educating the barbarian, now Eleonore giving
peace to the man dissatisfied with himself and
distrusting himself—mother, friend, confidant,
adviser. She was to me the ideal of a woman,
and she is my ideal even now. And I repeat it
here, that I did not lose myself in London, body
and soul, I owe in a great measure to her who
appeared to me like Leukothea to the ship-
wrecked Odysseus, when I thought I should
sink in the surging ocean of the misery of the
exile, and who gave me fresh courage to swim.

* * * * * * * * *

A STORMY CHESS MATCH.

Marx was an excellent player on the checker-
board. He had acquired such a dexterity at

this game that it was difficult to win a game from him. He also liked to play chess—but here his art did not amount to much. He tried to make up what he lacked in science by zeal, impetuousness of attack and surprise

In the beginning of the fifties, chess was played frequently in our society of fugitives; we had more time—and in spite of the adage "Time is money" less money—than was agreeable to us, and under the direction of the red Wolff, who had chanced to gain access to the best society of chess players in Paris and had learned something, the "Game of the Wise" was zealously cultivated. We had many a hotly contested chess match. The loser did not have to provide any derision; and even while the match was in progress, the hilarity was always great and sometimes very loud. When Marx was hard pressed, he lost his temper, and when he lost a game, he was furious. In the model lodging house of Old Compton street, where several of us lived for a time at 3 shilling 6 pence per week, we always were surrounded by a circle of Englishmen who watched our game—chess is much cultivated in England, particularly among workingmen—with great attention and were amused by our merry, noisy ways. For two Germans make more noise than six dozen Englishmen.

One day Marx announced triumphantly that he had discovered a new move by which he would drive us all under cover. The challenge was accepted. And really—he defeated us all one after the other. Gradually, however, we learned victory from defeat, and I succeeded in checkmating Marx. It had become very late, and he grimly demanded revenge for next morning, in his house.

At 11 o'clock sharp—very early for London—I was on the spot. I did not find Marx in his room—but he would be in immediately. Mrs. Marx was invisible, Lenchen did not make an over-friendly face. Before I could ask whether anything had happened Marx entered, shook hands and at once fetched the chess board. And now the battle began. Marx had studied out an improvement of his move over night, and it was not long before I was in a tight place from which I could not escape any more. I was checkmated, and Marx was jubilant—his good humor had suddenly reappeared, he ordered something to drink and a few sandwiches. And a new battle began—this time I was the winner. And thus we fought with changing luck and changing humor without taking time to eat, satisfying our hunger by hastily taking from a plate that Lenchen had brought us meat, cheese and bread. Mrs. Marx remained invisible, neither did any one of the children dare to enter —and thus the battle raged, surging up and down, until I had checkmated Marx twice in succession and midnight had arrived. He insisted on playing more, but Lenchen—the dictator of the house under the supremacy of Mrs. Marx—declared categorically: "Now you stop!" And I took leave.

Next morning, when I had just risen from my bed, somebody knocks at my door, and in comes Lenchen.

"Library"—the children had dubbed me thus and Lenchen had accepted this title, for the title "Mister" was not in use among us—"Library, Mrs. Marx begs that you play no more chess with Mohr in the evening—when he loses the game, he is most disagreeable." And she told me how his bad humor had vented itself so severely that Mrs. Marx lost her patience.

Henceforth I did not accept any more invitations from Marx to play chess in the evening. Chess playing, moreover, was forced to the background in proportion to our regaining regular occupations. As for myself who had acquired a certain reputation as a player in our little circle, I convinced myself in the course of time of the correctness of Lessing's criticism on chess: "For a play too earnest, for earnest too much play." I was invited by prominent players; and in the company of professionals I soon found out that the moves I had invented and of which I had been so proud had been discovered centuries before my time; I thus saw myself placed in the position of that farmer in the Pyrenees who had discovered anew during the reign of Louis Philippe the tower clocks that had already been discovered four centuries before. I learned that a voluminous literature on chess existed and that, if I expected to excel, I should have to study this literature and devote myself entirely to chess. And to take up chess as a vocation, I could not well make up my mind. So I gave it up. I have not played a game of chess since, but I delight in watching good players when I have the opportunity.

* * * * * * * * *

Speaking of this diplomatic mission of Lenchen, let me mention in this place that she was often employed in family missions, especially also in missions to the enraged head of the family. Since the foundation of the family in the house of Marx, Lenchen had become—as one of the daughters of the house expresses it—the soul of the house, and in the noblest sense a "maid of all work." Was there anything she did not have to do? Was there anything she did not do cheerfully? I will only remind you of the many trips to that mysterious, deeply hated and still assiduously courted, all-benevolent relative: the "uncle" with the three globes. And always cheerful, always ready to help, always smiling. But no! She could also become aroused and the enemies of "Mohr" she hated with grim hatred.

When Mrs. Marx was sick or ailing, Lenchen took the place of the mother—and always she was like a second mother to the children. And she had a will—a strong, hard will. What she deemed necessary, that was done.

* * * * * * * * *

Lenchen exercised, as I have said, a kind of distatorship—in order to define the relation correctly I should say: Lenchen had the dictatorship in the house, Mrs. Marx the supremacy. And Marx submitted like a lamb to this dictatorship. It has been said: No man is a hero to his valet. To Lenchen, Marx assuredly was not great. She would have sacrificed herself for him, for Mrs. Marx, for every one of the children, if it had been necessary and possible—and she has really given her life—but Marx could not inspire her with awe. She knew him with his humors and weak points, and she rolled him around her finger. His temper might be ever so exasperated, he might storm and thunder ever so much, keeping everybody else at a distance, Lenchen went into the lion's den, and if he growled she gave him such a severe lecture that the lion became meek as a lamb.

* * * * * * * * *

IN FIELD AND HEATH.

Our trips to Hampstead Heath! If I grew to be a thousand years old, I should not forget them. The "Heath" of Hampstead, beyond Primrose Hill, and like the latter known to the world outside of London through the Pickwick Papers of Dickens, is this day for the greater part a heath, that is, an undulating, uncultivated place covered with heather and clumps of trees, with miniature mountains and valleys, where everybody may move about and gambol at will without fear of being arrested and fined for tresspassing by a guardian of holy private property. To-day Hampstead Heath is still a favorite excursion place for Londoners, and on fine Sundays everything is black with male and multi-colored with female beings of the human tribe, the latter testing with special preference the patience of the admittedly very patient riding donkeys and horses. Forty years ago Hampstead Heath was much larger and much more natural and primeval than to-day. And a Sunday on Hampstead Heath was the highest pleasure to us. The children spoke of it the whole week, and we grown people, too, old and young, anticipated it with joy. The trip itself was a feast. The girls were good pedestrians, alert and tireless like cats. From Dean street, where Marx lived—a short way from Church street, where I had gone to anchor—it was at least one hour and a quarter, and as a rule the start was made as early as 11 o'clock a. m. Often, it must be admitted, we started later, for it is not customary in London to rise early, and some time was always consumed in getting everything in readiness, the children cared for and the basket properly packed.

That basket! It stands, or rather hangs before my mental vision as vivid, as real, as enticing, as appetizing, as if it were only yesterday that I had seen it last on Lenchen's arm.

It was our commissary department, and when a man has a healthy, strong stomach and very often not the necessary small change (large change did not come our way at all), then the question of provisions plays a very important

role. And good Lenchen knew this and had
for us often half-starved and, therefore, always
hungry guests a sympathizing heart. A mighty
roast veal was the center-piece hallowed by tra-
dition for the Sunday on Hampstead Heath. A
basket of a volume unknown in London, which
Lenchen had saved from their sojourn in
Treves, served as a receptacle to the Holiest of
Holies, as a tabernacle so to speak. After this
tea with sugar, and occasionally some fruit.
Bread and cheese was purchased on the heath,
where one could—and still can, obtain dishes
and hot water with milk, similarly to the coffee
gardens of Berlin, and bread, butter, cheese, besides the local shrimps, water-cress and peri-
winkles, according to one's needs and purchas-
ing power. Also beer—except during the short
time when the society of aristocratic hypocrites,
who have piled up at home and in their clubs all
the alcoholic drinks imaginable and to whom
every day is a Sunday or holiday, tried to im-
press virtue and morals on the common people
by prohibiting the sale of beer on Sundays.
But the people of London don't understand a
joke when an attack is made on their stomachs;
by the hundred thousand they wandered out to
Hyde Park on the Sunday after the passage of
that bill and thundered into the ears of the pious

aristocratic males and females, who were en-
joying their rides in carriages and on horseback,
a sneering "Go to church!" so loud that the pious
males and females were terror struck.   On the
next Sunday, the quarter of a million had increased to half a million, and the "Go to
church!" had become stronger and more serious.
And by the third Sunday, the measure was already revoked.

We fugitives had helped to the best of our
powers in this "Go to church!" revolution, and
Marx, who could grow very excited on such occasions, came near being collared by a policeman and dragged before a magistrate, but a
warm appeal to the thirst of the brave guardian
of the law was finally successful.

But, as I said, the triumph of hypocrisy did
not last long and, except during this short inter-
regnum, we could console ourselves on the almost shadeless march to Hampstead Heath by
the well-deserved and well-founded prospect of
a cool drink.

The march itself was generally accomplished
in the following order.   I led the van with the
two girls—now telling stories, now executing
callisthenics, now on the hunt after field flowers
that were not so scarce then as they are now.
Behind us some friends.   Then the main body

of the army: Marx with his wife and some
Sunday guest requiring special attention. And
behind these Lenchen with the hungriest of the
guests who helped her carry the basket.   If
more visitors were there, they took different
places between the several divisions of the
army.   That the order of battle or of march
was changed according to humor and need, I
will not emphasize.

Once arrived on the Heath, we would first
choose a place where we could spread our tents,
at the same time having due regard to the possibility of obtaining tea and beer.

But after drinking and eating their fill, as
Homer has it, the male and female comrades
looked for the most comfortable place of repose
or seat; and when this had been found, he or she
—provided they did not prefer a little nap—produced the Sunday papers they had bought on
the road, and now began the reading and discussing of politics—while the children, who
rapidly found comrades, played hide and seek
behind the heather bushes.

But this easy life had to be seasoned by a little diversion, and so we ran races, sometimes we
also had wrestling matches, or putting the shot
(stones) or some other sport.   One Sunday we
discovered a nearby chestnut tree with ripe

nuts: "Let us see who can knock down the greatest number!" somebody cried, and with a great uproar we went to work. Mohr behaved like mad, and the knocking off chestnuts was surely not his strong side. But he was untiring—like all of us. And only when the last chestnut had been captured amid wild shouts of triumph, the bombardment ceased. Marx could not move the right arm for eight days. And I was not better off.

The greatest treat was a general donkey riding. That was a mad laughing and whooping! And those ludicrous scenes! And how Marx amused himself and us. Us he amused twofold: by his more than primitive art of riding and by the fanatic zeal with which he affirmed his skill in this art. The skill consisted in having once taken riding lessons while a student—Engels contended that he had not gotten beyond the third lesson—and in taking a ride once in a score of years during his visits to Manchester in company with Engels on the back of a demure Rosinante, probably the great-grand-colt of the lamblike mare that the "old Fritz" had once upon a time given to the good Gellert.

The walk home from Hampstead Heath was always very merry, although a pleasure we have enjoyed does not, as a rule, awaken as agreeable feelings as one we are expecting. Against melancholy—although there were only too many good reasons for it—we were charmed by our irrepressible humor. The misery of exile did not exist for us—whoever began to complain was at once reminded in the most impressive manner of his social duties.

The marching order on the way home was different from that on the march out. The children had tired themselves out running and formed the rear together with Lenchen who, after the basket had been emptied, could take care of them with a light foot and light weight. Generally somebody started a song. Political songs seldom, mostly popular songs, especially sentimental songs and—this is no fish story—"patriotic" songs from the "fatherland"—for instance "Oh Strassburg, Oh Strassburg, Du wunderschoene Stadt" (Oh Strassburg, Oh Strassburg, you wonderful town") that was an extraordinary favorite. Or the children sang nigger songs for us and danced an accompaniment—if their legs had sufficiently recovered. Politics were tabooed on the march as well as the misery of exile. Literature and art, however, were much discussed, and there Marx had an opportunity to show his gigantic memory. He recited long passages from the "Divina Commedia" that he knew almost entirely by heart; and scenes from Shakespeare at which his wife, also an excellent student of Shakespeare, frequently relieved him. When in the highest of high spirits, he represented Seidelmann as Mephisto. He adored Seidelmann whom he had seen and heard in Berlin as a student, and Faust was his favorite German poem. I cannot say that Marx recited well—he exaggerated considerably —but he never missed the point and he always expressed the sense correctly—in short, he was effective, and the ludicrous impression caused by the first violent outburst of words soon passed when it became apparent that he had deeply penetrated into the spirit of the character, had fully grasped it and thoroughly mastered the role.

Little Jenny, the elder of the two girls (Tussy, alias Mrs. Eleanor Marx-Aveling, was then still in the lap of the future), the image of the father —the same black eyes, the same forehead—had sometimes prophetic Pythian raptures—"the spirit came over her," as it did over Pythia; her eyes began to shine and to flame, and she commenced to declaim, often the most singular fancies. On the way home from Hampstead Heath she once had such an attack, she spoke of the life on the stars, and what she said took the

form of a poem. Mrs. Marx, with the anxiety
of a mother who has lost several children, became alarmed and remarked: "No child of her
age should talk like that—this premature development is not a sign of health." But Mohr
scolded her, and I pointed out to her how Pythia, awakened from her trance, gamboled about,
laughing merrily—the picture of health. True,
little Jenny did die young—but the pain of sur-
viving her was at least spared to the mother.

With the increasing growth of the two girls
the character of these Sunday walks changed—
but a new generation being provided for, the
youthful element was never missing.

Several children died; among them Marx's
two boys, one, born in London, very early, the
other, born in Paris, after a protracted illness.
Well I remember the sad weeks of sickness
without hope. The death of this boy was a
fearful blow to Marx. The boy—named
"Moosh" (mouche—fly), really Edgar after an
uncle—was very gifted, but ailing from the day
of his birth—a genuine, true child of sorrow this
boy with the magnificent eyes and the promising
head that was, however, much too heavy for the
weak body. If poor "Moosh" could have obtained quiet, enduring nursing and a sojourn in
the country or near the sea, then, perhaps, his

life might have been saved. But in the life of the exile, in the chase from place to place, in the misery of London, it was impossible, even with the most tender love of the parents and care of a mother, to make the tender little plant strong enough for the struggle of existence. "Moosh" died; I shall never forget the scene; the mother, silently weeping, bent over the dead child, Lenchen sobbing beside her, Marx in a terrible excitement vehemently, almost angrily, rejecting all consolation, the two girls clinging to their mother crying quietly, the mother clasping them convulsively as if to hold them and defend them against Death that had robbed her of her boy.

And two days later the burial. Lessner, Pfaender, Lochner, Conrad Schramm, the red Wolff and myself went along—I in the carriage with Marx—he sat there dumb, holding his head in his hands. I stroked his forehead: "Mohr, you still have your wife, your girls and us— and we all love you so well!"

"You cannot give me back my boy!" he groaned—and silently we rode on to the grave-yard in Tottenham Court Road. When the coffin—singularly large, for during the sickness the formerly very backward child had grown surprisingly,— when the coffin was about to be lowered into the grave, Marx was so excited that I stepped to his side fearing he might jump after the coffin.

Thirty years later when his faithful mate was buried out on Highgate Cemetery, and with her half of his own being, his own life, he would have fallen into the grave, had not Engels—who later told me about it—quickly grasped his arm.

Fifteen months later he followed her.

* * * * * * * * *

Later on Tussy came, the little merry thing, round as a ball and like milk and blood—first in a perambulator, in America called baby carriage, then either carried around, or tripping along beside you—she was six years old when I returned to Germany, half as old as my oldest daughter who during the last two years also joined our Sunday trips to Hampstead Heath.

Like milk and blood she was, and so is to this day Tussy, now Mrs. Eleanor Marx-Aveling. And there are very good reasons for the "milk and blood," the knowledge of which may benefit a good many people.

Mrs. Marx had lost all her children born in London. When Tussy announced her arrival, there was held a grand consultation and the family physician, Dr. Allan, an excellent man whom Marx trusted implicitly, declared that there was only one possibility to keep the child healthy and alive, vizi.: to feed it on nothing but milk up to its fifth year, and mainly on milk up to its tenth year. And so it was done. Therefore it is not to be wondered at that Tussy became like milk and blood, for milk is blood. And many a human being could be like her, if it had such sensible parents.

* * * * * * * * *

When, from the beginning of the fifties, we lived in the North of London, in Kentish Town and Haverstock Hill, then our favorite walks were on the meadows and hills between and beyond Hampstead and Highgate. Here flowers were sought, plants analyzed, which was a two-fold treat for the city children, in whom the cold, surging, bellowing stone sea of the metropolis created a veritable hunger for green nature. What a joy for us, when we discovered in our wanderings a little lake shaded by trees, and I could show to the children the first live "wild" forget-me-nots. And still greater was the joy when we found hyacinths among other spring flowers in a sheltered corner of a luxurious meadows of dark velvety-green, which we had entered in spite of the warnings against trespassing after a careful scrutiny of the territory. I could hardly believe my eyes. The hyacinths—so I had learned—grow wild only in southern countries, in Switzerland on Lake Leman, in Italy, Greece, but not farther north. But here I had the manifest proof of the contrary and an unexpected testimony in favor of the English contention that England has an Italian climate for the vegetable kingdom. No doubt, they were hyacinths, simple blue-grey blossoms, not so many and so large blossoms to a stalk as there are on the garden hyacinth, but with a similar, only somewhat more intense odor.

I had learned in studying Homer that the asphodel-meadow on which the dead heroes took their walks, was a meadow of narcissi and hyacinths. And now our meadow between Highgate and Hampstead transformed itself into an asphodel-meadow, and we wandered among the hyacinths as happy as the blessed heroes and deemed ourselves more fortunate than Achilles, for we were alive, and with grim earnest the dead slayer of Hector had exclaimed in the hearing of the well-versed and much-wandered sufferer Odysseus:

Better to be a farmer on earth and to labor
for others,
Than to be king of the dead in the reign of
the shadows.

We were alive, and we did not have to look up longingly to the upper world—we looked proudly down on the world from our sweet-scented asphodel meadow—on the mighty, endless metropolis that is the world and extended before us immeasurable, wrapped in a nasty, mysterious cloak of fog.

* * * * * * * * *

A BAD QUARTER OF AN HOUR.

Who does not know the bad quarter of an hour of Rabelais—the quarter of an hour when accounts must be squared or even worse is threatening? And who has not had bad quarters of an hour? I had many a one. Before examination—before my first speech—the first time before the door of the prison when ordered by the attendants to deliver my suspenders and my necktie, in order that I might not evade the court-martial by suicide, as was explained to me with brutal frankness in reply to my perplexed question—those and many others were surely bad quarters of an hour. But compared to the quarter of an hour of which I am about to relate they were pleasant. It was not even a quarter of an hour. An eighth of an hour at the most. Perhaps only five minutes. I did not measure the time. I did not have time. And if I had had the time, I had no watch.

Fugitive and watch!   I only know that to me
it was an eternity.

It was on the 18th of November, 1852, and in
London.   The "Iron Duke" and "victor in a
hundred battles" whom the English people had,
nevertheless, made meek and tame at the time
of the reform movement—Lord Wellington had
died on the 14th of September in his Walmer
Castle, and on the 18th of November the "national hero" was to receive a "national burial"
and to be laid with "national" pomp in St. Paul's
Church alongside of other "national heroes."
Since the day of his death—nearly two months
past—this celebration had been the talk of all
England and especially of all London, for just
as the man who was the center of it had surpassed all former heroes in the opinion of Englishmen, so this celebration should surpass all
former national festivities in splendor and
grandeur.   And this was the day.   All England was in motion, all London was on foot.
Hundreds of thousands had gathered from the
provinces—thousands and thousands from foreign countries.   And the millions of the
metropolis!

I detest such spectacles, and I have always
had a horror of crowded masses of human beings,
and like most of my fellow-fugitives I had had

the intention to stay at home or to go to James Park. But two lady friends had upset my Catonic resolution—que femme veut, Dieu le veut—women's will is God's will, even if they are only 6 and 7 years old, like my two lady friends. Oh, we were such good friends, the dark-eyed, dark-haired Jenny Marx—with a head exactly like that of her father "Mohr"—and the graceful blond Laura with the roguish eyes—the joyous image of her beautiful mother who in spite of the bitter earnest of the exile could on certain occasions still smile as mischievously as the ever merry "Loerchen"—I repeat, we were extremely good friends, the two girls and I.

And the two girls, who from the first day of our acquaintance had attached themselves closely to me and always claimed me as their own when they caught sight of me, contributed in no slight degree to preserve in the London exile that cheerfulness to which I owe my life. Nothing cheers and strengthens more in such critical times than intercourse with children. How often, when I was at my wit's end, did I flee to my little friends and saunter with them through streets and parks! Then the gloomy thoughts were quickly dispelled, and with my good humor the buoyant strength to fight for my existence or for other things also returned.

Generally I had to tell stories—after a few days I became the chosen "story-teller" who always was received with enthusiasm. Happily I knew many fairy tales, and when my stock was exhausted, I had to compose fairy tales—this, however, did not succeed very long, for the bright girls soon found out, when I was serving up fragments of old stories as hash,— and so I finally had to invent new fairy tales. Thus I became through necessity, if not a poet, at least a manufacturer of fairy tales—until the "stories" were followed by history. And no one has ever had a more thankful, appreciative audience. But whither did I stray? I was going to describe my bad and worst quarter of an hour.

"Only take very good care of the children! Don't mix up with the crowd!" Mrs. Marx had said before dismissing us, when I left for the "show" with the impatiently tripping girls. And below in the vestibule, Lenchen who had hurried after us called out anxiously: "But be careful, dear Library!" Mohr who generally rose late had not been visible.

I had made my plan—money for renting a place in some window or some stand we had none—the pageant went along the Strand, followed the Thames. We would have to go to

one of the streets that enter the Strand from
the North, sloping gently toward the river.

With a girl on each hand, my pockets filled
with some lunch, I steered for the point of view
I had selected for us—in the vicinity of Temple
Bar, the old city gate separating Westminster
from the city. The streets, full of unusual stir
since early morning, were crowded with people;
but the procession having to traverse widely extended quarters of the giant city, the millions
scattered themselves and we arrived at my
chosen spot without being crowded. The place
proved to be entirely satisfactory. I posted myself on a staircase, the two girls clinging to
each other and standing on a higher step, while
I held on to one with each hand.

Hark! A stirring of the human ocean; a far-
off, increasing noise, like the hollow roaring of
the sea coming nearer and nearer! An "Ah!"
from ten thousand and ten thousand throats.
The pageant is here, and we can view it excel-
lently from our position, as if in a theater. The
children are delighted. No squeezing—all my
fears are dispelled.

A long, long time the gold-bedecked procession
takes in passing with the enormous, showy
catafalque bearing the "conquerer of Napoleon"
to his tomb. Always something new—always

and always—until it is all over.   The last gold-
laced rider has disappeared.

And now suddenly a shock—a storming for-
ward of the masses wedged in behind us. Every
one wants to follow the procession.   I resist
with all my strength, trying to protect the children so that the torrent will rush by without
touching them.   In vain.   Against the ele-
mental force of the masses, no human strength
will avail.   As well try to brave the shock of
ice after a hard winter in a frail canoe.   I am
forced to give way, and pressing the children
close to me, I endeavor to escape the main cur-
rent.   Already I have apparently succeeded and
I breathe more freely, when suddenly a new and
mightier wave of humanity rushes on from the
right; we are pushed into the Strand, and the
thousands and hundred thousands, who had
gathered in this great thoroughfare-artery, endeavor to rush after the pageant, in order to enjoy the spectacle once more.   Clenching my
teeth, I try to lift the children on my shoulders,
but I am jammed in too tightly—I seize the arms
of the children convulsively, the whirlpool drags
us away, and all of a sudden I feel a force
wedging itself in between the children and myself—I clasp one of their wrists in each hand—
but the force that has shoved itself between me

and the children forges ahead like a wedge—
the children are torn away from me, and—all re-
sistance is useless—I must release my hold, or
I would have broken or dislocated their arms.
It was a horrible moment.

What now? Before me rose Templebar Gate
with its three passages—in the middle for
wagons and horses and on the sides for pedestrians. Along the walls of this gate the human
flood, similar to the water on the pillars of a
bridge, had piled up—I had to get through! If
the children had not been trampled down—and
the agonized shrieks of fear rising on all sides
showed me the whole danger—then I hoped to
find them on the other side, where the pressure
would cease. I hoped! I exerted myself like
a madman, using my chest and my elbows.
But in such a turmoil a single man is like a
straw swimming in a whirlpool, I fought and
fought—a dozen times I thought I was in the
passage and was hurled aside. At last a shock,
a fearful squeezing—and in a moment I am on
the other side and free from the wildest throng.
I looked about, running hither and thither.
Nothing! My heart sinks within me—There,
two clear childish voices: "Library!" — — — I
thought I was dreaming. This was angelic
music. And before me stood, smiling and un-

hurt, the two girls. I kissed and hugged them. For a moment I was speechless. And now they told me how the human wave that had torn them from me had carried them safely through the gate and then cast them aside—under the shelter of the same walls that had caused the pressure on the other side. There they had posted themselves behind a projection of the wall, remembering my old instruction to remain on the spot or as near to it as possible, in case they should lose me on any of our excursions.

We returned home in triumph. Mrs. Marx, Mohr and Lenchen received us jubilantly, for they had been deeply apprehensive; they had heard that there had been an immense throng, and that many had been killed or hurt. The children had no idea of the danger through which they had passed—they had enjoyed themselves splendidly. And I did not mention that evening what a fearful quarter of an hour I had experienced.

In the same place where they had been torn from me several women had lost their lives, and the frightful scenes of that afternoon were largely instrumental in helping to break down Temple Bar, that abominable obstruction of traffic.

But to me that bad quarter of an hour is present as vividly as if it all had happened only yesterday.

And since that time I never went with children to a place where I anticipated a throng. And I shall never do so.

* * * * * * * * *

PATRIOTISM AND ITS CONSEQUENCES.

During the worst times of the exile we, nevertheless, had often a very merry time—of course only those who were fortunate enough not to die of starvation. We did not suffer from the blues. And if the world before us seemed shut off by a wooden wall, we adopted the device of the Sheffield workingmen: A short life and a merry one. But who thought of dying? Never say die! And often we reveled madly—the worse off the more reckless. There was only one remedy against the grinning misery: Laughter! Whoever indulged in gloomy thoughts was infected by the disease and swallowed. But before a ringing, merry peal of laughter, misery flies like the devil before the crowing of a rooster.

And this is the remedy which I recommend to all, for it is good and remains so as long as the globe lasts. Never did we laugh more than when we were in the worst circumstances.

And what did we not do in our reckless humor!

Sometimes it even happened that we relapsed into our old student's pranks. One evening Edgar Bauer, acquainted with Marx from their Berlin time and then not yet his personal enemy in spite of the "Holy Family," had come to town from his hermitage in Highgate for the purpose of "making a beer trip." The problem was to "take something" in every saloon between Oxford street and Hampstead Road—making the "something" a very difficult task, even by confining yourself to a minimum, considering the enormous number of saloons in that part of the city. But we went to work undaunted and managed to reach the end of Tottenham Court Road without accident. There loud singing issued from a public house; we entered and learned that a club of Odd Fellows were celebrating a festival. We met some of the men belonging to the "party," and they at once invited us "foreigners" with truly English hospitality to go with them into one of the rooms. We followed them in the best of spirits, and the conversation naturally turned to politics—we had been easily recognized as German fugitives; and the Englishmen, good old-fashioned people, who wanted to amuse us a little, considered it their duty to revile thoroughly the German princes and the Russian nobles. By "Russian" they meant Prussian nobles. Russia and Prussia are frequently confounded in England, and not alone on account of their similiarity of name. For a while, everything went along smoothly. We had to drink many healths and to bring out and listen to many a toast.

Then the unexpected suddenly happened.

"Patriotism" is a disease by which a sensible man is attacked only in foreign countries; for at home there is so much miserable inadequacy that everybody who is not suffering from paralysis of the brain or spinal meningitis is charmed against the bacillus of this political vertigo, also called chauvinism or jingoism, and most dangerous when those attacked by it sanctimoniously turn their eyes upward and carry God's name on their lips.

"In Saxony I praise Prussia, in Prussia I praise Saxony," said Lessing. And this is a sensible patriotism that tries to cure the defects of the home country by the example of the real or imagined good in foreign countries. I had taken advantage of this word of Lessing at an early period, and the only drubbing I received since the days of my youth was due to an attack of patriotism while I was abroad. It was in Switzerland. On a certain occasion, when in the "Haefelei" in Zurich, Germany was abused too violently, I jumped up and said to the gentlemen: "Instead of abusing Germany, you should be glad of the German misery, for to it alone Switzerland owes its existence. Once the table is cleared in Germany and over there in Italy and France also, Switzerland will cease to exist: German Switzerland will of itself revert to Germany, French Switzerland to France and Italian Switzerland to Italy." It was really a silly political forecast that I kept on tap there, but it was in the "mad" year and my patriotism had been aroused. My speech did not meet with a pronounced approval—as I could gather from the frowning miens of my hearers. I found violent opposition, but the conversation gradually slackened and—it had become rather late—I turned homeward. On the landing place, near my lodging, several forms suddenly appeared before me, and before I became aware of it, I was tripped—I fell down and before I could raise myself, I received several very hard blows, whereupon my opponents took to their heels. I have never found out who they were, but I did not doubt for a moment that my patriotic speech in the "Haefelei" had procured this anonymous drubbing for me.

And now in London, in the company of the kind old Odd Fellows, I together with my two companions "without a country" came into a quite similar position. Edgar Bauer, hurt by some chance remark, turned the tables and ridiculed the English snobs. Marx launched an enthusiastic eulogy on German science and music —no other country, he said, would have been capable of producing such masters of music as Beethoven, Mozart, Haendel and Haydn, and the Englishmen who had no music were in reality far below the Germans who had been prevented hitherto only by the miserable political and economical conditions from accomplishing any great practical work, but who would yet outclass all other nations. So fluently I have never heard him speaking English. For my part, I demonstrated in drastic words that the political conditions in England were not a bit better than in Germany (here Urquhart's pet phrases came in very handy), the only difference being that we Germans knew our public affairs were miserable, while the Englishmen did not know it, whence it were apparent that we surpassed the Englishmen in political intelligence.

The brows of our hosts began to cloud, similarly as formerly in the "Haefelei"; and when Edgar Bauer brought up still heavier guns and began to allude to the English cant, then a low "damned foreigners!" issued from the company, soon followed by louder repetitions. Threatening words were spoken, the brains began to be heated, fists were brandished in the air and— we were sensible enough to choose the better part of valor and managed to effect, not wholly without difficulty, a passably dignified retreat.

Now we had enough of our "beer trip" for the time being, and in order to cool our heated blood, we started on a double quick march, until Edgar Bauer stumbled over a heap of paving stones. "Hurrah, an idea!" And in memory of mad student's pranks he picked up a stone, and Clash! Clatter! a gas lantern went flying into splinters. Nonsense is contagious—Marx and I did not stay behind, and we broke four or five street lamps—it was, perhaps, 2 o'clock in the morning and the streets were deserted in consequence. But the noise nevertheless attracted the attention of a policeman who with quick resolution gave the signal to his colleagues on the same beat. And immediately countersignals were given. The position became critical. Happily we took in the situation at a glance; and happily we knew the locality. We raced ahead, three or four policemen some distance behind us. Marx showed an activity that I should not have attributed to him. And after the wild chase had lasted some minutes, we succeeded in turning into a side street and there running through an alley—a back yard between two streets—whence we came behind the policemen who lost the trail. Now we were safe. They did not have our description and we arrived at our homes without further adventures. In Marburg, a similar adventure had not taken the same smooth course for my comrades, and had also had some disadvantage for myself who had not been caught right away. Here in London, where they have no sympathy for German students' pranks, the matter would have been much more serious than in Marburg, Berlin or Bonn; and I must confess that on the next morning—no, at noon of the same day—I was very glad to be in my room, instead of being locked up in a London prison cell together with the member of the "Holy Family," Edgar Bauer, and the future creator of "Capital," Karl Marx. But we laughed whenever we thought of this night's adventure.

* * * * * * * * *

TOBACCO.

Marx was a passionate smoker. Like everything else, he carried on smoking with impetuousness. English tobacco being too strong for him, he provided for himself, whenever he had any chance of doing so, cigars which he half

chewed in order to highten the enjoyment or to
have a double pleasure. As cigars are very
dear in England, he was continually on the
hunt for cheap brands. And what kind of stuff
he secured in this way, may be imagined;" cheap
and nasty" is an English expression, and Marx's
cigars were consequently dreaded by his friends.
And with these abominable cigars he completely ruined his smoking taste and smell. He
nevertheless believed and contended that he was
an excellent connoisseur of cigars, until one
evening we laid a trap for him, into which he
unwarily fell. A visitor from Germany had
brought some fine imported cigars with him
during the year of the exposition of 1851, and
we began to light and smoke them with ostenta-
tious relish, when Marx entered. The unwonted
aroma tickled his nose. "Ah, that smells excellent!" "Well, these are genuine Havanas
brought over by X! Here, try one." And the
speaker offered to the guileless Marx, who de-
lightedly accepted, a specimen of the most horrible brand of cigars we had been able to find
in St. Giles, the worst proletarian quarter of the
West End, which brand resembled the genuine
article in form and color. The "horrible example" in the way of a cigar was lighted, Marx
blew the delicious smoke into the air with rap-

tured mien. "I was a little suspicious at first; generally they bring a miserable weed from Germany; but this one is really good!"—We assented with grave faces, although we were ready to burst. A few days later he learned the true state of things. He did not lose his temper, but maintained obstinately, that the cigar had been a genuine Havana and that we were now trying to hoodwink him. And he could not be convinced of the contrary.

Marx's passion for cigars had also a stimulating effect on his talent for political economy— not in theory, but in practice. He had smoked for a long time a certain brand of cigars that was very cheap according to English ideas—and proportionately nasty—when he found on his way through Holborn a still cheaper brand—I believe for one shilling and sixpence per pound and box. That brought forth his political-economic talent for saving: with every box he smoked he "saved" one shilling and sixpence. Consequently, the more he smoked the more he "saved." If he managed to consume a box per day, then he could live at a pinch on his "savings." And to this system of saving which he had demonstrated to us one evening in a humorous speech he devoted himself with so much energy and self-sacrifice that after the lapse of some months the family physician had to interfere and to forbid Marx peremptorily to enrich himself by such a system of "saving."

We had many a laugh over this Marxian theory of saving. That equally practical theories of saving would be believed in and seriously considered as a solution of the social problem by the "nation of thinkers" for many years—such a thing we did not suspect at that time. I learned this fact only after my return to Germany. In England, whenever similar allusions were made in English newspapers, I had always regarded them as inventions.

* * * * * * * * *

DISEASE AND DEATH.

Not being completely familiar with the last years of Marx's life and with sundry family affairs and occurrences, and finding it necessary to revive my memory in regard to several points, I applied to my ever-helpful, untiring friend "Tussy," I mean Mrs. Eleanor Marx-Aveling, for information—asking her to answer several questions. The answer came. More questions, further replies.

In the following notes I reproduce the information—given in English, for Tussy's mother-tongue is not that of her mother and father. Like all German children born in England she has preferred the easier English to the extremely difficult German. Of all the languages known to me, the German is the most difficult and the English the easiest, and for this reason English is most suitable for a world's language, especially since it has the distinction of being one of the richest, strongest, most expressive and most beautiful languages and being spoken even now by the larger half of civilized people —surely by more than German and French combined.

I know what difficulty I had in preventing my daughter, who was born in London, from forgetting, during her sojourn there, all the German learned at home. And Marx took great pains that his children learned German thoroughly— while I know some famous German "patriots," who when abroad banished German from their family circle.

But that children in England should show less liking for the far more difficult German than for English is quite natural and cannot, therefore, be prevented by the most rigid discipline. Thus it has come about that Eleanor Marx-Aveling writes German only exceptionally and when compelled to do so—although she speaks German perfectly, fluently and correctly.

* * * * * * * * *

About the sojourn of Mohr in Mustapha (Algiers) I cannot say much beyond that the weather was abominable, that "Mohr" found a very capable and amiable physician there, and that in the hotel everybody was attentive and pleasant to him.

During the fall and winter of 1881-82, "Mohr" was with Jenny first in Argenteuil, near Paris, Here they met us and we remained together for some weeks. Then he went to the South of France and to Algiers, but was very ill on his return. The fall and winter of 1822 he passed in Ventnor (Isle of Wight), whence he returned in January, 1883, after Jenny's death—January 8th.

Now to Carlsbad. We visited it for the first time in 1874. "Mohr" was sent there on account of a liver trouble and of insomnia. In the following year, that is 1875—his first stay had benefited him greatly—he went alone. The next year, 1876, I again accompanied him, because he said he had missed me too much the year before. In Carlsbad he used the treatment with utmost conscientiousness and did punctually everything that was prescribed. We made many friends there. As a traveling companion, "Mohr" was charming. Always in good humor, he was ever ready to enjoy everything, a beautiful landscape as well as a glass of beer. And with his extensive knowledge of history he made every place that we touched still more vivid, still more real in the past than even in the present.

I believe that several authors have written about "Mohr's" sojourn in Carlsbad. Among others I heard about a lengthy essay, but I do not remember the name of the publication; perhaps M. O. in D. can tell you more about it. He spoke to me of a very good article.

In 1874 we met you in Leipsic. On our way home that time, we made a flying trip to Bingen —which "Mohr" wanted to show me, because he had been there with my mother on their wedding trip. Besides we also went, during these two trips, to Dresden, Berlin, Prague, Hamburg, Nuremberg.

In 1877 Marx should again have gone to Carlsbad, but we were informed that the German and Austrian governments intended to expel him, and the voyage being too long and too expensive to risk being expelled, he did not go to Carlsbad any more—to his great disadvantage, for he always felt like one born anew after his treatment there.

To Berlin we went principally in order to see the faithful friend of my father, my dear Uncle

Edgar von Westphalen. We stayed only three days. To "Mohr's" relish we learned later that the police visited our hotel—just one hour after we had left it.

* * * * * * * * *

In the fall of 1880—our good "Moemchen" (little mother) was already so sick that she could rise only seldom from her couch of suffering. "Mohr" had a grave attack of pleurisy. It had become dangerous, because he had always neglected his trouble. The physician (our excellent friend Donkin) thought the case almost hopeless. It was a terrible time. In the large front room our little mother was lying, in the small room next to it "Mohr" was also confined to his bed. And these two, so much accustomed to one another, so closely allied to each other, could not be together in the same room any longer.

Our good old Lenchen (you know what she was to us) and I, we had to nurse them both. The physician said that our nursing had saved "Mohr's" life. Be that as it may, I only know that neither Lenchen nor I ever got into bed for three weeks. We were on our feet day and night, and whenever we were too much exhausted, then we rested alternately for an hour.

"Mohr" recovered from his sickness for this once. Never shall I forget the morning when

he felt strong enough to go into dear mother's
room. They were young once more together—
she a loving girl and he an adoring youth who
together entered on their life—not an old man
wrecked by sickness and a dying old woman
who took leave of each other for life.

"Mohr" grew better, and although he was not
strong yet, he seemed to be growing strong.

Then dear mother died—on the 2d of December, 1881; her last words—curiously enough in
English—were addressed to her "Karl."

When our dear general (Engels) came, he said
—what I then almost resented—:

"Mohr is dead too."

And it was really so.

With dear mother's life, "Mohr's" life went
too. He fought hard in order to keep up, for
he was a fighter to the last—but he was broken.
His general health became worse and worse.
If he had been more selfish, he would just have
allowed things to go as they pleased. But to
him there existed something that stood above
everything—that was his devotion to the cause.
He tried to complete his great work, and for
this reason he consented once more to a trip
for recreation.

In the spring of 1882—as mentioned before—
he went to Paris and Argenteuil, where I met

him; and we passed a few very happy days with Jenny and her children. "Mohr" then went to the South of France and finally to Algiers.

During his whole stay in Algiers, Nizza and Cannes he was troubled by bad weather. From Algiers he wrote long letters to me. Many of them I lost because I sent them to Jenny at his request;— and she returned only a few of them.

When Mohr finally came home, he was very ailing; and now we began to fear the worst. On the advice of a physician he passed the fall and winter in Ventnor on the Isle of Wight. In the spring of 1883 I went to "Mohr" and took with me Johnny for whom among his grandchildren he had taken a special liking. I had to go back because I had to give my lessons.

And then came the last terrible blow: the news of Jenny's death. Jenny, the first-born, the daughter that Marx loved most, died suddenly on the 8th of January. We had letters from "Mohr"—I have them before me now—telling us that Jenny's health was improving and we (Helen and I) need not worry. The telegram announcing the death arrived an hour after the letter in which "Mohr" wrote thus. I departed at once for Ventnor. In my life, I have had many sad hours, but none was as sad as this one. I felt that I was bringing the death-warrant to my father. On the long, fearsome way I had raked my brain how to impart the news. I did not have to impart it, my face betrayed me. Mohr said immediately: "Our little Jenny is dead!" and then he requested me to go at once to Paris and attend to the children. I wanted to assist him—he would have no contradiction. I had hardly been half an hour in Ventnor, before I returned on my dreary, sad way to London, going from there immediately to Paris. I did what "Mohr" had wished to be done for the children.

I pass over my return trip—only with horror can I recall that time—that anguish, that torture —let me dismiss it. Enough—I returned and "Mohr" came home—to die.

And now a last word of dear mother. She was dying for months and suffering all the horrible tortures incidental to cancer. And in spite of this, not a moment did her good humor, her inexhaustible wit, forsake her. She inquired impatiently, like a child, for the results of the contemporary elections in Germany (1881), and how she rejoiced at the victories! She was in good spirits up to her death and tried to dispel our fears for her by joking. Yes, she—who suffered so terribly—she joked—she laughed— she laughed at us all and at the physician, because we were so grave. Nearly up to her last moment she retained her full consciousness, and when she could not speak any more—her last words were addressed to "Karl"—she pressed our hands—and tried to smile.

As to "Mohr," you know that he went from his bedroom to his study in Maitland Park, sat down in his armchair and quietly fell asleep.

This armchair the "general" had up to his death, and now I have it.

When writing about "Mohr," don't forget Lenchen, whatever you do. I know you will not forget dear mother—Helen was so to speak the axis around which everything in the house revolved. The best and most faithful friend. Therefore do not forget Helen, when writing about "Mohr."

* * * * * * * * *

And now to your question in regard to our good Helen or "Nymy," as we used to call her last, because Johnny Longuet called her so (I don't know why) while he was a baby. As a little child of 8 or 9 years, Lenchen came to my grandmother von Westphalen and she grew up with "Mohr," dear mother and Edgar von Westphalen. For the old Westphalens, Lenchen always entertained a great affection. And so did "Mohr." He never tired of telling us of old

Baron von Westphalen and of his wonderful knowledge of Shakespeare and Homer. He could recite whole rhapsodies of Homer from beginning to end, and most of the dramas of Shakespeare he knew by heart in English and German. "Mohr's" father on the other hand— "Mohr" greatly admired his father—was a genuine Frenchman of the 18th century. He knew his Voltaire and Rousseau by heart, as the old Westphalen knew his Homer and Shakespeare. And the astonishing variety of Marx's accomplishments was undoubtedly due in a great measure to these "hereditary" influences.

But to resume regarding Helen. Whether she came to my parents before they went to Paris or after (which took place very soon after their marriage) I cannot say. I only know, that my grandmother sent the young girl to my mother "as the best she could send, the faithful, dear Lenchen." And the faithful dear Lenchen stayed with my parents, and her younger sister Marianne also followed later. You will hardly remember her, as that was after your time.

And now about our Scotch descent. It is so complicated that I never was able to determine it accurately. I know that we are closely related to the Argyle family through our great-grandmother. In connection with the Argyles you might tell an anecdote about "Mohr" that has never been published. In the first years of his stay in London, he once saw himself obliged to go to a pawnbroker—no rare occurrence during the exile. He brought some of the very beautiful and valuable silverware of my mother. There were especially some heavy silver spoons of different patterns—some 300 or 400 years old and all of them with the crown of the Argyles and their family device: "Truth is my maxim"—a fine device for the abominable family of the Campbells (to which the Argyles belong. The pawnbroker was so perplexed on seeing such rare and costly silverware in the possession of such a wild looking foreigner with bristling black whiskers that he wanted to have "Mohr" arrested, who escaped arrest only with great trouble and within a hair's breadth. His address was carefully noted and doubtless the police also made the necessary investigations. At any rate they must have been satisfactory, for no matter how often other silver spoons with the same crest went the same way later—no more difficulties followed after.

You ask if my grandfather was baptized before "Mohr's" birth? I believe so—but I cannot affirm it. The reason why the 18th century disciple of Voltaire submitted to such a ceremony was that otherwise he would not have been permitted to practice as a lawyer. And he was a lawyer when "Mohr"—the second child—was born. You will know that "Mohr's" mother, nee Pressburg, was a Dutch Jewess. In the beginning of the 16th century, the Pressburgs—taking their name from the town of Pressburg—migrated to Holland, where the sons of the family were Rabbis for centuries. "Mohr's" mother spoke Dutch; up to her death she spoke German faultily and with difficulty.

* * * * * * * * *

A VOYAGE OF DISCOVERY.

When I went to England in May of this year (1896), I resolved, after fulfilling my duties as an agitator, to make, before returning, a voyage of discovery into those parts of the city where we once had our abode as fugitives—and especially to search for the apartments of the family of Marx.

It was on the 8th of June—a Monday—when we started in the morning from Sydenham: Tussy Marx, Aveling and I, in order to reach by railroad, hack and omnibus the corner of Tottenham Court Road in the vicinity of Soho Square. Here the work of discovery began; and we went to work methodically—like Schliemann intending to excavate Troy. For our work was of a similar order and really not easy. He was going to excavate the Troy of Priam and Hector,—we the London of the fugitives from the close of the forties to the fifties and sixties.

The Troy sought by Schliemann had been buried three thousand years—the London sought by us for less than half a century. But the Greeks of the Trojan horse, with their childlike instruments of murder and destruction, were also harmless and weak pigmies in their knowledge of destruction, compared to the modern architects, engineers and speculators that to-day tear down and build up within a few days, what formerly could not be torn down and erected in many years, yes in decades.

What revolutionary changes in the modern great cities. It is a continual uprooting—although, as in political revolutions also, not everywhere, not in all parts. And a man starting to-day from a modern great city on a tour of the world will not be able on his return to find his way through a good many quarters. I remember how I fared when I returned to London in 1878, for the first time after an absence of sixteen years. I rubbed my eyes; was this the city in which I had lived for nearly half a generation and of which I then knew every street, every corner? Some things were still

as of old—but how much was new and strange!
And even the familiar objects changed by the
strange surroundings. Streets gone, sections
disappeared,— new streets, new buildings, and
the general aspect so changed that in a place
where I formerly could have found my way
blindfolded I had to take refuge in a cab in
order to get to my near goal.

Well, here we are at the corner of Tottenham
Court Road—in close proximity of Soho Square
and Leicester Square where the German and
French fugitives had herded together in a feeling of solidarity bred by loneliness.

We first wandered to Soho Square. Nothing
changed. The same houses, the same soot on
the houses, yea, even partially the same names
of firms on the sign boards. It was like a
dream. My youth rose before my eyes; forty
years, forty-five years disappeared like a misty
cloud blown away by a gust of wind—and as a
fugitive twenty-five years old I crossed the
Square, passing into one of the old well-known
side streets—Frith street or Greek street to Old
Compton street, where the old model lodging
house is still standing in which a generation
and a half ago we passed such boisterous,
hilarious and desperate times. Did not the

red Wolff flit by there Was not Conrad Schramm standing over there?

Everything as if I had been here only yesterday. It is miraculous! in this ocean of houses, London, there are streets and quarters which time passes by without leaving an impression, that remain untouched by the rushing waves of progress.

The storms outside there do not penetrate to this place—as once upon a time the storms of the French revolution roared on above wide strata of the population without as much as a stir of the quiet air,— without even causing the trembling of a single hair.

Everything as of old! Time has made a halt. Such must be the emotions experienced on witnessing the opening of a Pharaoh's tomb. The past has become the present—the present a past.

But let us go farther!

Here Dean street where Marx lived.

We do not enter yet. First to Church street and to Macclesfield street.

Right—there is the church—giving Church street its name—unchanged. The unavoidable public house opposite the church—unchanged. And here the three-story, grey-black houses with two front windows—unchanged. Involuntarily

I felt for my latch key.   But the door was ajar.
And here No. 14 where I had lived eight years
—unchanged.

I entered the vestibule, glanced up the stairs
to the second and third stories where I had
been quartered alternately—then down the stairs
to the kitchen, where I have asked many a time
for grace from the good landlady and her daughters when the amount I owed for rent had
reached too high a figure.

But away!   London is large and we are just
at the beginning—yes, at the beginning of the
beginning only.

Back and around the street corner: there is
Macclesfield street.   Only a few houses.   No.
1, 2, 3, 4, 5—where is No. 6?   Is this really
Macclesfield street?   It is—and it is not.   Here
the house must have been standing.   In vain
we look about—here is a new street—the house
in which Engels had spread his tent in the beginning of the London exile, until he was sent by
his stern parent to Manchester into the family
business—it has been swallowed by the new
street.   And the public house, in which I with
Engels and Conrad Schramm had once sung a
song that might have softened stones for the
delectation of the English regular guests, who
rewarded us with a stormy applause—it has be-

come a large gin palace. Only the hardware
store of the good Mr. Tozer whose name may be
found to this day on some relics of my knives, is
still there, quite unchanged—the firm alone is
another.

And now I look around me—new streets—ne\
names of streets. Everything overthrown.
And the new larger, more beautiful than the
old. Dudley street and St. Giles, where the
misery huddled together—swept away. The
slums and dens and rookeries—all gone. And
neat clean streets. The moral and "respectable"
society has had an attack—not of decency, but
of "moral blues," and in this attack it has been
ashamed of itself, and in order to avoid having its sins always under its nose and in its
nose, it has swept away the filth—swept it to
some other place, as lazy housekeepers and
housemaids sometimes carefully sweep the
refuse and rubbish in a room into a heap and
then convey it under the bed or into a hidden
corner. Only out of sight!

Was it not yesterday that Lord Shaftesbury
had "cleaned" London, removed the dens of vice
and misery and "lastingly" improved the condition of the unfortunate seamstresses?

Was it yesterday?

Yesterday? When was I here last? When

did I come from Switzerland and France? Yes
—Robert Peel who abolished the taxes on grain,
had just fallen with his horse and broken his
neck. It was in June, 1850. Forty-six years.
And to-day? Are the slums, the dens and the
rookeries abolished? Yes—in one place, but
they are in another. Just as bad, just as horrible as of old.

And the social evil? The "social evil," that is
prostitution discreetly so labeled. Has it
ceased to exist? Not in the least. Has it de-
creased? Twenty thousand prostitutes more
than at that time.

And the seamstresses? Has their condition
improved? Has the sweating system ceased to
flourish? No, no! The number of victims has
increased, and if Hood were to rise from his
grave, he could add a few more verses to his
"Song of the Shirt." "Sweating" is in use more
than ever. And the sweating system has made
the tour around the world, like once the tricolor.

And could anything else be expected? No
man can get out of his skin. Nor can society
do so. You cannot ask of capitalist society
what it cannot accomplish; and it is incapable
from its very nature to exterminate the misery
and vice that it creates itself. It may—in moments of self-deceit—have the best intention in

the world—and Lord Shaftesbury surely had the good intention and also wealth, influence and power—it gets no farther than to good intentions, or if they become deeds, these deeds are only empty nutshells. The good will is nothing—Buckle has shown that already. And against the fact that effects last as long as the cause is in force, no single individuals, no group of men and no human class can successfully struggle.

The dens of vice and misery may be destroyed by society—that is a question of money and masons;—but as long as vice and misery exist they will, if expelled from one den, immediately look for another and surely find it.

Mere charlatan cures! Mere Penelope work! "Plowing the sea" the Englishman calls it. To draw a furrow through the water—nothing is easier. But over the furrow the waters close again, and the plowing has been in vain.

On! Now to Dean street. To search for the house in which Marx and his family lived for many years. Once before I had tried to find it, but had been unable to locate it accurately— and Engels had told me later that the numbers of the houses had been altered. The houses there resemble one another like so many eggs; and the time for a longer investigation had always been missing on my former stays in London. Lenchen, with whom I had spoken about this matter shortly before her death, had not been able either to locate the house with certainty. And Tussy who had been only a year old when the change of domicile from Dean street to Kentish Town took place, could, of course, not remember anything.

We had to proceed methodically. In the street, very little had been changed. Among the houses on the right side—counting from Old Compton Street—there were several, completely resembling each other on the outside, between which the choice was doubtful. The only fixed mark I had was a theater obliquely opposite toward Old Compton street. This theater, then a private theater belonging to a Miss Kelly, had been reconstructed since that time. To-day its name is Royalty Theater, and it is now much larger and wider, so that in consequence, as I did not know whether the enlargement had been made towards the right or the left, the only fixed point I had was somewhat out of line. Finally I got so far that I hesitated in my choice between two houses only. And now the outer aspect did not suffice any more—I had to penetrate into the interior. The door of one house was ajar. I entered: the staircase seemed familiar to me; the whole building arrangement, so far as I could see it from the floor, agreed with my recollections. But most of the houses in London are built on a pattern and factory-like plan and are entirely wanting in individuality and originality. I ascended to the first floor, and now I was no longer at home—everything appeared strange to me.

In the meantime Marx's daughter and her husband had made further investigations in the street. I communicated to them the doubtful result of my observations.

To the next house, then! It bears the number 28. Was my memory deceiving me? Did not Marx's house have that number? Yes,—for now I suddenly remembered that I had retained this number in the beginning of my stay in London by a mnemo-technic trick as being the double of my own house number. Then Engels must have been mistaken when he said the numbers had been changed. Had he only expressed a conjecture? We rang the bell. A young woman opened the door. We asked, if she remembered the former occupants and owners of the house.

Oh yes, but only nine years back.

Had she heard of a Mrs. Kavenagh (the

mother of a well-known female author), the landlady of the house in our time?

No!

Would she permit that I enter and inspect the house?

Certainly!

And she showed me upstairs herself.

The staircase was right. So was the whole plan, and the farther I went the more familiar things seemed to me. The steps leading to the back room—everything was right.

Unfortunately the rooms of the second floor, where Marx had lived, were closed. But as far as I could see everything tallied exactly. Doubt after doubt dissolved, until I was certain: here Marx has lived.

And when I came down, I exclaimed: "Found! this is the house!"

Yes, this is the house! The house where I have been a thousand times, the house where Marx—assailed, lacerated, gnawed by the misery of the exile and by the most furious hate of heartless enemies shunning no calumny— wrote his "Eighteenth Brumaire," his "Mr. Vogt," his letters to the New York Tribune, now at last collected under the title: "Revolution and Counter-Revolution," and where he

made his enormous preliminary preparation for
"Capital."

Here it was, where Mrs. Marx after the death
of one of her children born in London, of little
"Foexchen," in 1852, wrote with her heart's
blood on a loose sheet of paper:

"My grief was so great. It was the first child
I lost!"

And on the same sheet—added some years
later:

"Alas! I did not suspect, then, what was in
store for me, before which everything else
would sink into nothingness!"

She is speaking of the death of poor "Moosh."

A few months after Foxy's death little Fran-
ciska died. And on one of the loose diary
leaves, found only recently on sifting the papers, we read:

"On Easter of the same year—1852—our poor
little Francisca died of severe bronchitis.
Three days the poor child was struggling with
death. It suffered so much. Its little lifeless
body rested in the small back room, we all
moved together into the front room, and when
night approached, we made our beds on the floor.
There the three living children were lying at
our side, and we cried about the little angel who
rested cold and lifeless near us. The death of

the dear child fell into the time of the most bitter poverty. * * * (The money for the burial of the child was missing.)—I went to a French refugee living in the vicinity who had visited us shortly before.

He at once gave me two pounds sterling with the friendliest sympathy. With this money the little coffin was purchased, in which my poor child now slumbers peacefully. It had no cradle, when it entered the world, and the last little abode also was for a long time denied to it. What did we suffer, when it was carried away to its last place of rest!" * * *

We retire before this Niobe-grief, and before this heart-rending picture of the misery of exile.

Every word would be a detraction, yes, a desecration.

I should not have permitted this anguished cry of a tortured mother's heart to reach the light of publicity, if I had not received especial sanction from her daughter, Mrs. Eleanor Marx-Aveling, who publishes one of these diary notes in the preface of the English edition of "Revolution and Counter-Revolution."

And I had still another reason. About Marx innumerable lies have been told—and also this: that he lived in sumptuous state, while the rank and file of the refugees about him hungered

and starved. I do not think myself authorized
to enter into further details here, but this I can
say: what is once more vividly brought before
my eyes by those diary leaves, is not a solitary
case of want, such as anybody may meet with,
especially in a foreign country where points of
recourse are scarce; the misery of exile lasted
for years in its most acute form for Marx and
his family. And even in later days, when his
income became larger and more regular, the
family of Marx was not exempt from cares of
subsistence. For years,—and then the worst
was already over—the pound sterling Marx received every week for his articles to the "New
York Tribune" was the only certain source of
income. * * *

Before we leave the house in Dean street, let
me mention that Marx, when he came to London
in June, 1849, first had a lodging in Camberwell
—where, I have not been able to ascertain yet.
There he had some trouble in consequence of
the landlord's declaration of insolvency, the
creditors having the privilege to re-emburse
themselves with the furniture of the occupants,
according to English law; and the family of
Marx had then moved, in June, 1850—about the
time of my arrival in London—to Dean street,
after a short stay in a family hotel on Leicester

Square; in Dean street they remained for about seven years, until they moved to Kentish Town in the then still comparatively rural North of London.

* * * * * * * * *

In Dean street we had no further business now—we returned to the corner of Tottenham Court Road and took seats on a Kentish Town omnibus.

In Tottenham Court Road only few changes had occurred. The character of the street is still the same as ever—frequently still the same stores and firms.

To our left a chapel—the tabernacle of the Quaker Whitfield—wholly unchanged. Only the church yard is now closed. Under the stones there poor Moosh is buried and, I believe, the two other children who died as babies.

We approach Kentish Town. There that public house seems familiar to me. Right, it is the old Red Cap—so called from the picture of a girl with a red hood (Red Riding Hood). Here it was where we came within an ace of receiving a most unromantic drubbing on account of our romantic attempt at delivering a hard pressed Donzella out of her imagined distress.

Then "Mother Shipton"—another public house with the sorceress of that name as a devise—on the Prince of Wales Road. And opposite of Mother Shipton my old lodging—quite unchanged, as if I had left the house No. 3 Roxburgh Terrace only yesterday. But the name of the street is changed—I believe that group of houses is now counted in with Prince of Wales Road—and the number of the house is altered.

So far the omnibus has brought us. And now we turn on foot into Maldon Road. How I feel myself at home there! But only for a short while—soon I find streets that were not there when I left London. Where formerly was partly field, there dense masses of houses are now standing.

Aud suddenly Tussy lifts her arm and points to a house rather roomy for the conditions in a London suburb: "There it is!"

And sure enough—there it is—this is the house, or rather the cottage in Grafton Terrace, in which Marx lived to within ten years before his death. Here the little balcony, whence Mrs. Marx, reconvalescent from a severe attack of smallpox, used to greet her three daughters who lived in my house during her sickness.

The cottage had then the number 9, now it is No. 46.

Not far from there is No. 41 Maitland Park Road. Until nine years ago the house had the number 1. There Karl Marx died. After the two eldest girls had married, the family, finding the first house too large now—1872 or 1873—had moved hither.

In this whole section, nearly everything was new to me. Here the city had been at an end formerly, and during the thirty-four years elapsed since my time, the city of millions has far, far outgrown its old limits.

Silently we wandered out to Hampstead Heath, where much is changed, but still the old aspect is not effaced. We visited the old places, and finally, in order to gain strength for the long, tedious journey home,—a voyage through all England is not half as tiresome and fatiguing as a voyage through London—we took some refreshments in Jack Straw's Castle, so called after the castle Jack Straw had built for himself in the English child's primer.

Jack Straw's Castle! How many hundred times had we been here! And in the same room where we were sitting to-day, I had been sitting—long, long ago—dozens of times with Marx, with Mrs. Marx, with the children, with Lenchen and others.

And the past returned.

(THE END.)